# PERFORMING UNDER PRESSURE

"Performing in the Peak Zone is what sets records and wins prizes. But more importantly it's what helps each of us to redefine the limits of our own possibilities. The prize is the thrill of breaking through what we thought were our frontiers of achievement. This book sets forth the challenge and gives us solid guidelines for achieving them."

PETER THIGPEN, PRESIDENT, LEVI-STRAUSS U.S.A.

"Bob Kriegel has developed a very useful and effective means for teaching us how to deal with stress and to perform optimally under pressure."

LARRY GERSHMAN, PRESIDENT MGM/UA TELEVISION GROUP

"I strongly believe in the concept of the Peak Zone. I knew the world wasn't limited to just Type A's and B's. The ideas in this book are inspiring to a person like me who has a strong desire to keep improving. *Performance Under Pressure* makes a valuable contribution to personal excellence."

J. GARY SHANSBY, CHAIRMAN OF THE BOARD AND CEO,
THE SHAKLEE CORPORATION

"Beyond the frenetic 'Type N' personality and the laid back 'Type B' the authors describe a more attractive option. Their 'Type C' is a much needed model of what Hemingway once called 'Grace Under Pressure.'"

MARILYN FERGUSON, AUTHOR, *THE AQUARIAN CONSPIRACY*

"Intuitively, I have been practicing peak performance under pressure for years. It's exciting to see Bob Kriegel bring these ideas together into a clear and articulate conceptual framework."

JOHN SCULLEY, FORMER PRESIDENT AND CEO,
APPLE COMPUTER, INC.

"Bob Kriegel captures the essence of our daily bouts with pressure, performance, stress, and anxiety and offers us a healthy alternative to driving beyond our limits or passively watching life go by with little satisfaction. He teaches us how to increase the frequency of those moments of excellence, joy, and excitement so that we can be at our best more often."

David Jamieson, Ph.D. President,

American Society for Training and Development

"This book provides clear guidance on how to be effective and balanced in this overwhelming age of information. I think it should be required reading for all executives, entrepreneurs, and people who want to be productive."

Ms. Lee Berglund, Designer and Chairperson,

Personal Resource System, Inc.

# PERFORMANCE UNDER PRESSURE

## Being at your best when it counts!

From New York Times Bestselling Author
**Bob Kriegel, Ph.D.**

*This book is dedicated with love and respect to Edith K. Kriegel and Myrtle H. Harris.*

# ACKNOWLEDGMENTS

Our friend Anne Herbert wisely suggested that books should be published with a masthead like magazines and newspapers. We agree. They are rarely the work of one mind or heart. The following is the masthead for this book: people to whom we are deeply grateful for their assistance, encouragement and loving support.

—Gail Kriegel for her keen writer's mind and sharp editor's pencil which had a major impact on the book. Gail inspired and encouraged us throughout and showed us how to work together on this project.

—Curt Berrien, Richard Leifer, Mark Rosenblatt, Kristin Shannon, Deborah Ward and Linda Weinreb for their thoughtful and valuable feedback on the work in progress.

—Kay Goldstein and JeanA Warner for their willingness to work odd hours and last minutes.

—Rik Jadricek for making our computer "user-friendly" and us computer-literate.

—Dr. Tom "Zeke" McCord for his assistance constructing the Performance Zone Profile and his great sports stories.

—Jay George for his enthusiasm and help in organizing the test scores and footnotes.

—John Brockman, our agent, for his sound advice and support.

—Sara Alexander, Lee Amate, David Brandt, Laurie Brandt, Ken Dychtwald and Naomi Remen for their suggestions, love and support.

—All of the people who have attended our seminars over the past twenty years whose participation helped us learn about the Peak Zone.

—To all of the peak performers who took the time to be interviewed and were frank enough to share some of themselves with us.

—Otis Kriegel for his understanding of our late-night and weekend work sessions, and his thoughtful suggestions. For his enthusiastic support, his many hugs and the spark and humor and love he provides to our home and office.

*Until one is committed, there is hesitancy, the chance to draw back, always ineffectiveness, concerning all acts of initiative (and creation). There is one elementary truth the ignorance of which kills countless ideas and splendid plans: that the moment one definitely commits oneself, then providence moves too. All sorts of things occur to help one that would never otherwise have occurred. A whole stream of events issues from the decision, raising in one's favour all manner of unforeseen incidents and meetings and material assistance which no man could have dreamed would have come his way. Whatever you can do or dream you can, begin it. Boldness has genius, power and magic in it. Begin it now.*

**GOETHE**

# CONTENTS

# 1

# THE PEAK ZONE

## GETTING IN THE ZONE

One of the first speeches I ever gave was to 350 managers for a major telecom company. I panicked! The largest audience I had ever presented to was about 25. My heart was racing, my palms sweating, and my mouth felt like the Sahara.

But early in that speech, everything seemed to change. I experienced calmness in the midst of my excitement. The group was paying rapt attention, taking notes, nodding at all the right times, and laughing at my jokes. I felt like I had them in the palm of my hand and could do no wrong. I was floating. The standing ovation put the cap on it all.

There's nothing like that feeling when you're really 'on' in a pressure situation. It's an incredibly exhilarating experience. The right responses seem to come at the right time, and you respond perfectly to whatever arises. You're at the top of your game, doing more and better than you thought possible, and it feels effortless. There are lots of names for this type of experience—being in the zone, on a roll, in the flow, channeling.

We've all had those times when we got on a roll, were more productive with less effort, and completely in tune with what we were doing. At these times you feel great, on top of everything. Though you are more effective, it feels as if you aren't working nearly as hard as usual and feel full of energy.

## IN SPORTS

Getting into what we call that 'Peak Zone' can happen anywhere at anytime, but it often happens during a pressure situation when there is a lot on the line, because at these times, you are more motivated, focused, and intense. Often, it is in a sport when, for no apparent reason, you are playing over your head, time seems to slow down, and whatever you are doing feels effortless. Skiing "out of your mind" is what we used to call this experience in our Inner Skiing clinics. On these runs, your body just seems to take over, and you feel as if you are flowing down the slopes in perfect harmony with the mountain. It sometimes happens for a few holes in golf when much to your surprise and delight you are driving the ball farther and straighter and sinking putts. And it all feels easy._

## AT WORK

United States Senator Barbara Boxer describes the experience as "... being on a roll, I feel confident and enthusiastic and everything seems to work. I am able to accomplish a great deal with a minimum of effort. My energy keeps building and gets transferred to whomever I am working with."[1]

Tom Simpson, who became president of Norwegian Caribbean Cruise Lines at thirty-three and doubled their revenues within three years, says that sometimes during what would ordinarily be very tense negotiations, "... I am able to stay relaxed and feel as if I am not trying as hard as usual or pushing and yet I am much more effective."[2]

My brother Doug, an Emmy Award-winning TV news reporter for NBC in Los Angeles has to research a story, write the copy, get it shot and edited, and do the commentary, all in the space of a few hours. He says, "Sometimes when I'm rushing to meet a deadline, I become so involved and focused on what I am doing that I'm unaware of anything going on around me. I get calm and everything becomes easy. It's unbelievable. I've done my best work at these times."

These high-performance episodes can be experienced in many different ways. It can be openness and calm when learning a difficult new skill; aggressiveness and daring when confronting a challenge; energy and expansiveness when talking to a large group. It can produce the extra energy needed for handling a sudden overload situation; the presence of mind to give each call your full attention when all the buttons on your phone are blinking and your e-mails are dropping on you like a snowstorm; or the intense concentration and concern for detail you need when preparing a complex report.

# HIGH PLATEAU

Being in the zone isn't that rare peak experience that comes once in a lifetime when you get lucky. It isn't some far-off nirvana that can be reached by meditating for hours and forsaking all other endeavors. It's a high plateau of optimal-performance behavior we all have experienced at various times in our lives and can learn to experience again. The qualities most inherent when in this zone are the following:

**Transcendent**. You are much more effective and productive than usual. You break your own records.

**Effortless.** You perform better without "trying so hard," or straining. Whatever you are doing feels easier than usual.

**Positive.** You are optimistic. You have confidence. You feel good about yourself and what you are doing.

**Spontaneity**. You feel as if there is a natural flow between your thoughts and actions. Choices come easily and automatically.

**Focused**. Your concentration is intense. You feel totally involved and   connected to what you are doing and to the people you are working with. You often don't notice time flying by.

**Vitality**. Your energy level is high, which gives you a feeling of joy and wellbeing. You feel healthier and more alive.

# THE PEAK ZONE: SYNERGY IN ACTION

In our research we discovered that the three main characteristics that help people get into the zone are **a passionate commitment, confidence**, and **concentration**. These traits are inherent in us all of us though developed to different levels and expressed in different degrees, depending on the situation. But being in the zone isn't a result of any single one of these qualities; it is determined by the interrelationship of all three. In other words, you can be confident, but not focused, or really passionate but scared out of your wits.

But synergy occurs when you are confident about what you are doing, strongly committed and passionate about it, and feeling totally focused. The behavior or performance that results when this interaction occurs is that you do more than you thought you could and are more than you thought you were. The experience is similar to when the musicians in an orchestra are playing in perfect harmony; the result is a symphony transcending the sum of the sounds of each instrument. None of these characteristics is more important than another when performing in the Peak Zone. Your confidence, commitment, and concentration, like the instruments of an orchestra, work in harmony with each other to make whatever you are doing seem like beautiful music.

## CHOICE OR CHANCE?

Joan A., the marketing manager for a consumer package goods company, told of a time when she was in the zone. It was her first annual budget review with the CFO for her company whom she had never met. "I had to present my yearly plans, projections and an operating budget. I had heard he that he was real tough, a strictly 'by the numbers' person and I was worried because I had a lot of conjecture in my marketing plan. The topper was that when I got to the meeting, the CEO of the company was there as well as the VP of marketing. I'm not real great at making presentations at the best of times and I almost had a heart attack when I saw them all sitting there.

"But for some reason I felt calm and composed once I started talking. I wasn't intimidated as I normally would have been. I seemed to know their concerns before they voiced them and had the perfect answer out of my mouth without even thinking about it. I was amazed at how I was responding to their questions; I sounded so confident. When I left the office, I was floating. I not only got what I asked for but they told me they were so impressed with my plans that they gave me a 10 percent increase in my budget request. If I could be like that in every meeting I'd be the hottest executive in town."

When we asked Joan why she thought this happened, she shrugged her shoulders. "I don't know. I was well prepared but I'm always well prepared for meetings, especially important ones like that one. Usually I get very intimidated in pressure situations but for some reason—I still can't figure it out—I was really 'on' for that meeting. It just seemed to happen."

Most of the time, as with Joan, getting on a roll happens by chance. For no apparent reason, you suddenly get hot in a tennis match and play way over your head. Or "out of nowhere," the work you have been struggling to finish just starts flowing. It can happen when you are feeling confident or when you are scared and tense. Sometimes, this experience occurs when you are well prepared, other times, when you are "winging it." Yet in most cases, this high performance episode seems to happen by accident. So people often attribute it to luck, hoping that it will strike again soon and often.

## WHY?

Why are these high performance episodes so elusive? Why do they seem to come and go so quickly? Why is it that we can go from breakthrough to breakdown within the space of two runs on the ski slope? Or hit a great drive on one hole and duff it on the next? Is there a way to be in this peak zone more often? What do you need to do to achieve and sustain a high level of performance?

In the early 1970s, a group of us at the Esalen Institute Sports Center, one of the first organizations to explore the mental side of sport, were researching "peak experiences" and developing innovative ways to help people learn more easily and perform at their max. We originally thought that being in the zone was  an experience that could be reached and repeated when need be. Many books have been written on the subject since that time, perpetuating this idea, and motivational speakers regularly pitch this promise.

Much to our dismay, after having worked with many elite

athletes and leaders in all fields, we found that no one seems to be able to get into that peak zone on purpose, by choice rather than chance. And no one performs in his or her peak zone even most of the time. Sometimes, even Tiger not only blows putts in a major tournament, but even misses making the cut. LeBron and Kobe have subpar games. And even the biggest stars of stage and screen have off nights.

But one difference between great clutch performers like these and everyone else is that, when under pressure, they seem to perform at their best more often and for longer periods of time than most people. The frequency, duration, and intensity of their peak zone episodes are greater because they have developed methods, techniques, and a mindset that enable them to get into this high performance state more often.

The techniques outlined in this book and the Performance Zone map will help you to learn how to make high performance episodes happen more often when you really need them. They will still happen by chance when you least expect them, but the more you practice these techniques, the easier it will be to perform at your best and to reach that high performance plateau more often by choice rather than by chance. As golfing legend Ben Hogan once said, "The more you practice, the luckier you get." Though Hogan was talking about golf, his advice is just as applicable for your mindset.

The Peak Zone isn't the province of a chosen few. We all can learn to experience our own personal potential more often and as a result do more than we imagined we could and be more than we thought we were. Nobel laureate Albert Szent-Györgyi pointed out that all humans have a natural tendency to expand and make the most of their potential. The goal of this book is to enable you to tap into your latent potential to experience and express yourself more fully. It is to turn that potential into performance wherever you go and with whatever you are doing.

Take a moment now, and do the following exercise:

1. Recall and describe in detail a time when you were in the zone.
2. What were you feeling at that time?
3. What was going on in your mind?
4. What was the experience like physically?
5. What were the qualities you expressed at these times (for example, confidence, courage, power, poise, charisma)?
6. Imagine performing in the zone, expressing these qualities in a high-pressure situation coming up. See it in your mind's eye. Experience it as fully as possible.

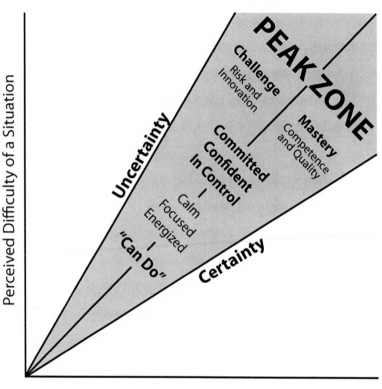

Perceived Difficulty of a Situation

Perceived Ability to Handle a Situation

PEAK ZONE

Challenge
Risk and
Innovation

Mastery
Competence
and Quality

Uncertainty

Committed
Confident
In Control
|
Calm
Focused
Energized
|
"Can Do"

Certainty

# 2
# THE PERFORMANCE TRIANGLE

## THE PERFORMANCE TRIANGLE

There are three components to any activity: Skills, Strategy, and State of Mind. Maximizing each leg of this triangle is the key to performing in the Peak Zone. Since most of us experience giving speeches or big presentations as extremely stressful, I am using this experience as the example for explaining what I call the performance triangle.

## STRATEGY—INFORMATION

It is obviously critical to understand your topic and your audience—who they are; what they do; their goals, challenges, current situation, past experiences, agendas, and biases. Knowledge of the audience is critical for customizing your presentation and connecting with them. You also have to be clear about what you want to achieve in any presentation—whether it is to make a sale, get buy-in for an idea, or to motivate and entertain—and to have developed a strategy for achieving this goal. This might include tools such as Power-Point, slides, video, and/or handouts.

Strategy in a sport involves knowing everything you can about your opponent and having an action plan for any given situation. In golf, for instance, strategy would be knowing the right club to use in a certain situation. In tennis, it might be how to get your opponent to come to the net.

## SKILLS

You obviously must have the appropriate skills to implement your strategy and achieve your goals. If you can't hit a drop shot in tennis, you probably won't get your client to come to the net. And if your goal is to entertain a group and you are a lousy joke teller, for instance, you are in trouble.

Body language, eye contact, tone of voice, and movement are some of the basic presentation skills. It is also important to know how to make the physical space complement the style of presentation you're giving. As an example, I always set up the stage before a speech, which includes a podium on the side so that I can move around, stairs in the front so that I can walk in the audience, and having house lights up, which helps me to see them. I have also found that people have more energy in a well-lit room. I also prefer to have either a lavaliere mike or a headset, as opposed to a hand-held mike so that I can have freedom to move my arms.

# STATE OF MIND

The third component of the performance triangle is your mental state, both before and during the event. Your state of mind consists of how passionate, enthusiastic, and energetic you are. It also involves your level of confidence, composure, and self-control, which includes learning to conquer and manage fear, stress, nervousness, and doubt.

# "BASS ACKWARD"

Most of us tend to spend most of our preparation time focused on the information and skills we need to make the presentation a success. We make sure we're up to speed on the data we need and our specific goals. Then, we make doubly sure that we have the appropriate support, such as Power-Point, slides, video, or handouts.

There are plenty of materials available—books, training programs, and coaching programs—that focus on these two aspects of a presentation. They teach you how to organize your material and how to use high-tech tools to deliver it. They explain the importance of developing skills, such as making eye contact with all parts of the room, modulating your tone of voice, determining how and where to stand, how much and where to move, and of not hiding behind the podium. One program I attended spent a whole segment on what not to do with your hands—never put them in your pockets. Men should never use the fig-leaf pose—holding your hands in front of your fly, and women were cautioned not to fiddle with their hair.

To be sure, strategy, information, and skills are critical for the success of any presentation, but focusing primarily on these aspects is a case of the tail wagging the dog. In a disastrous presentation (described in the next chapter) I once made to Procter & Gamble's management when I was working in advertising, I had all the information I needed, as well as terrific visuals, support materials, and handouts, and I'd rehearsed until I could deliver the information in my sleep. But it wasn't wasn't lack of information, support material, or prep time that caused me to blow it. It was my nervousness— my state of mind caused me to bomb.

It's It's the same in any presentation, large or small. You can have the most up-to-date, mind-boggling data, the most innovative ideas, plus great visual aids, but if you're you're too nervous, you won't won't communicate effectively. A stressed state of mind can cause you to rush over, or even forget, important points and make mistakes. You might talk too fast or have major eye blur—not making eye contact with anyone.

Fear and nervousness can also do the reverse and sap your energy or cause you to hide behind the podium, speak too softly and tentatively, and simply bore the people you're trying to sway. And if you aren't passionate and enthusiastic about your message, you'll be dull, lack energy, and the loudest sound you'll hear from the audience will be snoring.

# THE MENTAL GAME

The importance of state of mind to performance is very visible in sports. What causes a pro golfer to miss a three-foot putt, as Sergio Garcia, ranked sixth in the world, did on the 18th hole of the '06 U.S. Open, with the match on the line? He wasn't lacking skill and practice—he'd made that shot a thousand times. He was nervous and choked. And he isn't the only pro to have turned a potential birdie into a devastating bogie. The same is true for us weekend duffers. We can look great on the driving range, but we don't seem able to replicate those shots on the course. Why? Pressure affects our state of mind, which causes us to tighten up, hindering our ability to make shots.

As former golf pro Tommy Bolt said, "The mind messes up more shots than the body." And nervousness and stress not only affect you physically, but also mentally. Los Angeles Laker coach Phil Jackson, who has won more NBA championships than any other pro basketball coach, said, "In a close game, I check my pulse. I know if it gets over one hundred, it's it's going to affect my thinking."[1] The bottom line for effective presentations, as in golf, any other sport, or anything you do, is that your state of mind both before and during the presentation will determine how well you perform—how effectively you communicate the information you have, how well your audience receives it, and whether you achieve the results you want. Speaking about the relationship of the mind to skills, Tiger Woods says, "The mind controls the body...It's a matter of getting the mind under control."[2]

# POWER BASE

A reason that state of mind is the base of the performance triangle is that it's the underpinning of the total performance. Just as with a building, the strength of the foundation will determine the strength of the structure. If the base is weak, the structure is more liable to collapse.

Your state of mind is your power base. Your level of confidence, composure, control, and passion will determine how effectively you communicate your information, execute your skills and ultimately whether you motivate and inspire people.

This book's goal is to help you maximize each component of the performance triangle so that you can be at your best mentally, physically, and emotionally and perform in the Peak Zone more often.

# 3
# THE PEAK ZONE—FROM MASTERY TO CHALLENGE

When in your Peak Zone, you are constantly shuttling back and forth between mastery and challenge. Mastery is achieving competency or expertise at what you are doing. Challenge is upping the ante and playing for higher stakes by taking the risks necessary to get you to the next level. This mastery/challenge shuttle is a natural process through which you learn and grow in everything you do throughout your life.

Moving from mastery to challenge is like climbing a ladder, a familiar metaphor for achieving success. In this ascent toward the top, mastery, the achievement of competency, provides you with a strong footing and a solid base. Mastery involves remaining on a rung until you have your balance and feel confident, comfortable, and in control.

The challenge comes when you commit yourself to taking the risk of moving up to a higher step. Initially, you feel shaky at this new height. At this point, you strive for mastery, to gain balance and confidence until you are once again ready for the next challenge. The mastery/challenge shuttle, as can be seen in the diagram, takes you from the excitement of exploring the unknown to the satisfaction and fulfillment of a job well done. It shuttles you from uncertainty to certainty and back and keeps you learning, growing, and moving up the ladder.

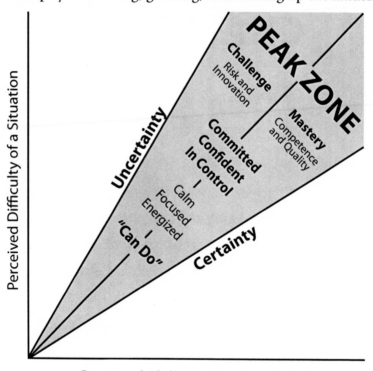

The late Dr. Willie Unsoeld, the first American to reach the summit of Everest, once told me, "You need an element of risk, a challenge to perform at your peak. The right amount of risk throws you into a state of total concentration where there is nothing but the moment. You feel as if you have more time and more strength to accomplish things than you ever thought possible. But before you take that risk, you've got to master the fundamentals and become competent in the technical aspects of what it is you are doing."

Describing this mastery/challenge shuttle, Tom Simpson told us, "I love challenging myself. There's a certain exquisite tension when you are on your edge. I feel drawn to the front lines. However, before I put myself out there, I always try to know as much as possible about what I am doing."

## CREATIVITY AND SPONTANEITY

The Peak Zone shuttle between mastery and challenge is a vehicle not only for growth and improvement but for creativity and spontaneity as well. The best comedians and speakers who interact spontaneously with their audiences, salespeople who can adapt a presentation on the spur of the moment, anyone adept at thinking creatively on his or her feet—all usually have mastery of their material in common. Mastery frees each of them to accept the challenge of the moment and to respond spontaneously, often with a surprising creativity.

Wynton Marsalis, the great jazz musician, sounds as if his playing is all improvised in that moment, and it often is. But underneath that spontaneity, Marsalis, like many other improvisational jazz musicians, has been classically trained since childhood and has practiced his art diligently. We can look at the paintings of Jackson Pollock and think, "Heck, he just dribbled paint on the canvas; anybody can do that." But Pollock's great leaps of creativity, which was also true of

Picasso and other modern artists, is that like Marsalis, they were all classically trained.

The same is true in sports. We see basketball stars such as Lebron, Kobe, Michael, and many others make some unbelievable moves and dunks. But for every move on the court that looks spontaneous and daring, they have spent hours practicing in the gym and schoolyard.

I have given more than 1,800 keynote speeches and, based on something I see occurring with the audience, I will often veer spontaneously from my notes to tell a story, use an example, or even go off on a new tangent. But before that spontaneous episode, I have prepared that speech until I have it down cold. That practice, the mastery part, gives me the confidence to take the risk and get off my track with something spontaneous.

The immortal golfer Ben Hogan once said, "The more you practice, the luckier you get." The same is true with spontaneity and creativity; the more you practice and learn, the greater and more creative your leaps will be. Creativity, as the saying goes, is 90% perspiration and 10% inspiration. And the perspiration has to come before the inspiration.

## EXPERIENCING CHALLENGE AND MASTERY

We have all experienced both aspects of this challenge/mastery shuttle:

### Challenge

Take a moment to reflect on several times in your life when you challenged yourself and took a risk in any area of endeavor.

Remember the excitement and anticipation of trying something that was new, uncertain, and a little out of your control. Remember how it felt—the energy, the fear, how vital and alive you were feeling, how your concentration sharpened, and how you experienced everything with more intensity.

Make a list of some of the risks you've taken. As you list them, remember them in as much detail as you can. Experience the challenge as fully as you can.

Now, make another list of several challenges you would like to take in the future, areas in which you are considering taking a risk.

## Mastery

Take a moment, and think about areas of your life in which you have achieved mastery or are extremely competent. Reflect on the feeling of satisfaction you derive from doing something well. Experience the ease and confidence with which you go about this work.

List several areas in your life in which you have achieved mastery, become competent or expert. Once again, as you write each down, reflect on how it feels to note your accomplishment.

Now, list a few areas in your life in which you would like to develop more competence and expertise.

# 4

# THE PANIC AND
# DRONE ZONES

Unfortunately, the zones we play in aren't always peak-performance zones. There are three performance zones: the Peak Zone, the Panic Zone, and the Drone Zone. Each zone encompasses a different type of behavior.

We have all experienced the shuttle from mastery to challenge and back that characterizes Peak Zone behavior. Most of us, however, gravitate toward either challenge or mastery. Some people devote most of their energies to honing their skills or increasing competence in one area. They enjoy competence and control. The excitement of a challenge draws others more. They love to take risks and explore new territories.

But the person who always overcommits and continually takes risks, is like the skier who constantly takes slopes that are too difficult. Sure, it's exciting, but if you never take the time to master the fundamentals, eventually, you'll take one risk too many and end up in your Panic Zone.

On the other hand, if you concentrate solely on increasing your competency and mastering the finer points of a task, you'll eventually come to a place of diminishing returns. The skier who has the ability to move up a level, but continues to ski the same slopes, will stop improving. Eventually, he will lose his enthusiasm, become lethargic, and end up in the Drone Zone.

## THE PANIC ZONE

If being in the Peak Zone is like a dream, being in the Panic Zone is a nightmare. We talk too fast, forget important points, don't make eye contact with anyone, and our minds go blank when someone asks an important question.

I had one of these Panic Zone experiences when I was the account executive on a Procter & Gamble (P&G) account for Young & Rubicam Advertising. It was the annual budget meeting at which we had to justify our recommendations for the coming year and defend our performance for the prior one. A lot rode on the meeting, like keeping the account for another year and, of course, keeping our jobs. Not only were P&G's top marketing people there but, since this was a major account, the agency's senior management was there as well.

Our account team had spent about three months preparing for the meeting. The handout we developed made the *Oxford English Dictionary* look like a paperback. As the major presenter, I had rehearsed for any question that might come up and had prepared 3x5 cards to help me with the pertinent facts and keep on track.

Despite all this preparation, I was in a panic before the meeting. My palms were sweaty; my throat felt as if someone had poured Sahara sand in it; and my heart was pounding so hard, I thought it was going to rip through my shirt. Looking at the assembled group only made it worse. They looked like they were starving, and I was the meal.

In an attempt to loosen them up and calm myself down, I started with a joke. Big mistake. Have you ever tried to tell a joke when you were nervous? It went over like the proverbial lead balloon. Everyone was now staring impatiently at me, and my boss was angrily giving me the "let's get moving" sign. Gulping, I looked down at my carefully ordered 3x5 cards and discovered that, in my panic, *I was nervously shuffling them!* Needless to say the presentation was painful for everyone.

Panic Zone experiences are enough to keep you off the dais and in the audience forever.

## TRYING TO DO TOO MUCH IN TOO LITTLE TIME

Because they are highly motivated, many people in our rapidly changing, increasingly competitive, results-oriented society overcommit and over challenge themselves. They take on too many responsibilities or inordinately high risks and get in over their heads and out of control. Trying too hard to do too much in too little time, they drive themselves into their Panic Zone.

In the Panic Zone, you experience great bursts of energy, but that energy is fueled by panic. Your stress is off the charts, and you are out of control. Your mind is racing; your concentration jumps from one thought to another with the speed of a strobe light, causing you to dart around frantically and fruitlessly.

The experience is like playing tennis with someone who is much better than you are but whom you desperately want to beat. You scramble from one side of the court to the other to retrieve a shot, your adrenaline pumping, your heart beating wildly. Then, before you can catch your breath, your opponent hits it to the other side of the court. You race over, just manage to return it, and she hits it well out of your reach again—and off you go....

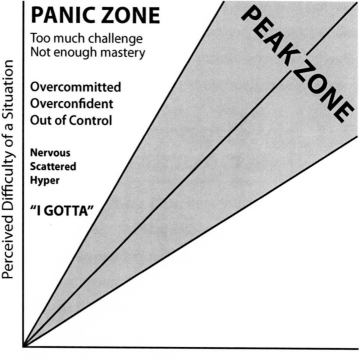

# IN THE WORKPLACE

What does the workplace look like when employees are in the Panic Zone? Very much like a henhouse with a fox lurking nearby. Everyone's running around in a frenzy, trying to do too much in too little time. People are nervous, pressured, irritable, and scared. They can't maintain focus and don't think clearly. Forget quality. People in a rush make more mistakes.

Creativity? No way.    People in the Panic Zone are reacting, not reflecting. Racing and rushing, they're unlikely to come up with a brilliant or inventive plan. They just do the same old, same old a little faster. Communication also suffers. It's hard to be clear, concise, and rational when you're racing around from one crisis to another.

In response to the question; "How are you trying to improve as a manager?" Dany Levy, founder and editorial director of DailyCandy.com, responded with a description of Panic Zone communication;. "Sometimes, I don't slow down enough to walk someone through why I'm making a decision about something… (and) I'm definitely a lot more impulsive and irrational."[1]

When in your Panic Zone, you're not in control of a situation, but reacting to it. You have no time to plan, to develop creative strategies, to problem solve effectively or to master any skill. You waste all your energy racing to get that ball that is always out of reach or to accomplish the task that is more than you can handle.

Time is the enemy when in the Panic Zone. When you're operating in this zone, you hate waiting and become impatient and irritable when anyone takes too long to complete a job, answer a question, or even finish a sentence.

Dr. Kenneth Pelletier, a leading authority on stress in the workplace, says, "The time pressures inevitably leave (this person) frustrated, nervous, hostile, and even more firmly determined to step up his efforts to accomplish more in less time. His struggle with the clock is a never-ending exercise in futility."[2]

The irony of being in your Panic Zone is that although you use achievement as a justification for this behavior, you usually don't achieve nearly what you are capable of. Dr. Pelletier amplifies, "In his eagerness to get things done as fast as possible, this person may respond to challenges in a rote manner, causing him to make errors in judgment. And since he never takes time to consider new approaches to, or implications of, a situation, his creativity will be inhibited."[3]

Though it might be hard to measure the cost in terms of performance, when you are in the Panic Zone, it's not hard to measure the cost of this type of behavior to life itself. Drs. Meyer Friedman and Ben Rosenman, who coined the term "Type A" to discuss this type of behavior, concluded that the Type A is three times as likely to develop heart disease than their less driven colleagues. Panic Zone behavior often results in the stress-related diseases now recognized as major causes of mental and physical illness, premature aging, and death in our culture.

## GETTING THE GOTTAS

The Panic Zone style most prevalent in today's high-pressure work world starts with a "Gotta" attitude. "I gotta make this deadline!" "I gotta make this sale!" "I gotta finish this report!" "I gotta be the best!"

The "gotta" attitude will sometimes provide a quick boost of energy. However, the stress and tension resulting from trying to do more in less time so that you can come in under deadline or over quota is counterproductive. In a Panic Zone rush to get a job done, you will often misread a situation, make hasty decisions, and act too quickly.

Discussing the "gotta cycle" in one of our seminars, Bill J., a manager for a large computer software manufacturer, said he saw no alternative. "After all, I gotta get the work done!"

Bill's response is one that comes up in every seminar when Panic Zone behavior is discussed. "What am I to do?" asks the typical Panic Zoner. "I don't have any choice!"

But, as has been discussed, your performance in the Panic Zone is usually poor, not reflecting your actual ability level. You don't think clearly when rushing; you don't take time to think something through, and as a result, you make more mistakes. To make matters worse, you don't communicate well and are usually short-tempered with your peers or staff.

On the rare occasions when this Panic Zone approach works, the extra effort and stress resulting from a "gotta" attitude has probably exhausted you and thrown your schedule into disarray. You are now in no shape to get to the next meeting or to tackle the next job. You need a breather to get organized. But you can't take too long a break because then you'll be that much more behind for your next project. Then, you "gotta" get that one done too.

There's a Catch-22 in the "gotta" attitude that makes it hard to change. If you do manage to accomplish your goals with this approach, you learn from experience that you "gotta" rush and work longer hours in order to succeed. On the other hand, if you don't succeed with this approach, you learn that you've "gotta" try even harder next time. Either way you remain in the Panic Zone and eventually the "gottas" gets you!

## THE DRONE ZONE

On the opposite end of the performance map is the Zone of the Drone. In the Drone Zone, resources exceed the challenges. Drawn to mastery, the Drone becomes very competent at what he is doing but never risks losing control by taking the next step. Because of the lack of challenge, his job becomes predictable, routine, and dull, and he loses interest in it and the motivation to perform well and go the extra mile. The Drone Zoner has ample skills to handle the task, but his lethargic attitude and lack of motivation causes him to perform poorly.

Jonathan L. was a family counselor for a big public utility in the Southwest. "When I first started this job, I loved it, and couldn't wait to get to work in the morning. The work was fascinating and challenging. But I've been doing it for three years now, and I'm bored. It's the same old routine day in and day out. It gets so I can't tell one person from the next anymore. And what's worse, I don't care. I know that I'm not doing as good a job as I used to. I feel like I'm on automatic. I can't get out of my office fast enough at the end of the day. I know it's terrible, but I don't know what to do."

Drone Zoners want to progress and make a move because they are bored and often hate what they are doing, but the fear of failing at the next level prevents them from taking a risk. So,

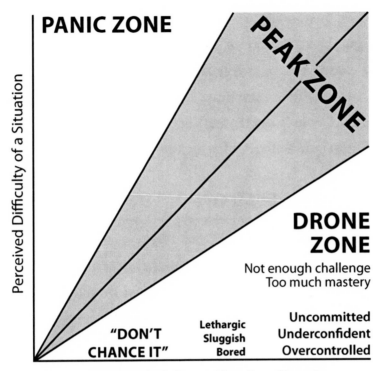

PANIC ZONE

PEAK ZONE

Perceived Difficulty of a Situation

DRONE
ZONE
Not enough challenge
Too much mastery

| "DON'T CHANCE IT" | Lethargic Sluggish Bored | Uncommitted Underconfident Overcontrolled |

Perceived Ability to Handle a Situation

they remain where they are, safe but sorry. "I'd like to open my own office," Jonathan continued, "and I know I'm good enough, but it takes a while to get started and develop a good practice. And there's no guarantee that I'll succeed. I've gotten used to making good money here. I'd hate to give that up for something that I'm not sure will work out. I feel stuck."

## BLUE RUNS

We would often encounter skiers coming to our Inner Skiing programs who were frustrated about their lack of improvement. It usually turned out that they kept skiing only those runs on which they were comfortable and in control. Their fear of falling or not looking good prevented them from challenging themselves to ski the next level. As a result they ended up in the Drone Zone, which hindered their improvement and caused lack of energy and enthusiasm. It's wonderful to be comfortable at something, but if you stick too long in your "comfort zone" like these skiers, eventually, you get bored and stop improving and having fun.

## MISSED OPPORTUNITIES

Companies end up in the Drone Zone when their leadership avoids challenges and stays glued to the status quo. Think of all the giants who became dinosaurs because they kept doing the same old, same old. The most obvious examples are the big three American car companies who rode high on their tail-finned gas-guzzlers with the oversized grills and engines. They got stuck by the roadside like an old junker making the same kind of car every year, while the rest of the auto world was changing in high gear. But they are only one of a multitude of companies who missed great opportunities. Just to name a few—IBM missed the personal computer, Xerox missed the personal copier, Kodak missed digital, and the list goes on of companies who believed in the status quo while the world around them was changing.

The Drone Zone might feel safe, but it's not free of stress. It's a different kind of stress from that experienced in the Panic Zone. When there don't seem to be any options, you become frustrated and depressed. This kind of negative stress is just as dangerous to your health and well-being as Panic Zone stress, resulting in disappointment and many of the depression-based illnesses.

# THE CAN'TS

The Panic Zoner thinks, "I gotta." The Drone Zoner's attitude under pressure is "I can't," and then he has a multitude of reasons that reinforce that thinking. As a result, he sticks with the status quo, taking few risks and resisting anything new. Then, if he acts, he does so tentatively, expecting and ensuring poor performance. "I was right," he thinks, "it was too difficult." His lack of confidence has been reinforced. The Drone Zoner, like the golfer faced with a 4-foot putt who thinks, "Don't over hit it," and ends up short putting, will often play it safe so as not to lose, which creates losing.

The difficulty of the task isn't the cause of the Drone Zoner's poor performance. It is his "I can't" attitude that results in failure and, therefore, becomes self-fulfilling. (See chapter on vicious cycles.)

# GETTING TO THE PEAK ZONE

No one remains in one zone all the time. We move from one to another, sometimes with amazing speed. You might even operate in the Panic Zone in one area of your life and the Drone Zone in another. Many people I encounter in my work are rushing, racing, and running in their desperate struggle to keep up, but in this mad rush, they're just responding in the same old way and repeating what they have done before. Therefore, they end up in both the Panic and Drone Zones simultaneously.

We do, however, tend to favor one zone more. Our personalities gravitate toward challenge and the Panic Zone or mastery and the Drone Zone.

To uncover your own peak potential, it's necessary to become aware of whether you tend to favor mastery or challenge and to what extent. The Performance Zone Profile in the next chapter will help you recognize your strengths and weaknesses and the zone in which you tend to operate. This information will aid in developing strategies for unblocking your innate abilities so that you will stay in your Peak Zone more often and for longer periods.

## USING THE ZONE DIAGRAM

You can use the Performance Zone Diagram to determine the zone in which you will operate for a specific task.

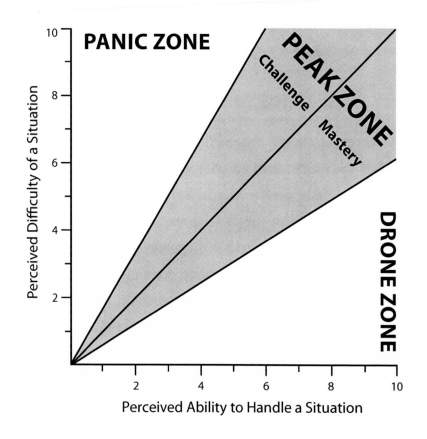

First, mentally rate your perception of the difficulty of the task on a scale of 1–10. Try to be as objective as possible. Draw a horizontal line across the diagram at the level you have chosen. Next, rate your perception of your ability to handle the task on the same 1–10 scale. Draw a vertical line from the point you have chosen.

The spot where the two lines intersect will indicate which zone you expect to play in during that particular task. If you are taking a risk or challenging yourself, your performance point should be slightly to the left of the center line, in the challenge area of the Peak Zone. If, on the other hand, you are performing a job at which you are competent, you should end up slightly to the right of the center line, in the mastery area.

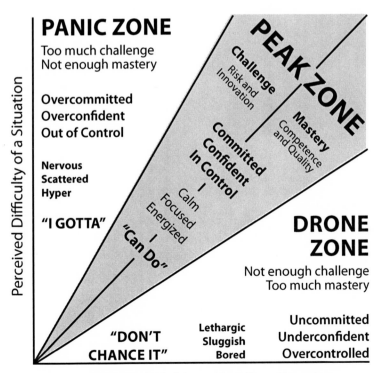

If you end up too far to one side or the other, in either the Panic or Drone Zones, you need to rethink your expectations and goals or up the level of your skills.

# 5
# THE PERFORMANCE ZONE PROFILE

To determine your predominant performance zone, we have developed a short diagnostic test, the Performance Zone Profile, which requires about a half-hour to take and score. Your test score will indicate your strengths and weaknesses, as well as the performance zone you favor. This information will enable you to identify more easily, and subsequently overcome, the obstacles to performing at your peak.

## TAKING THE TEST

Focus on your performance in a specific area. Answer each question honestly. Circle the number that most accurately describes your behavior as it is, not as you would like it to be or think it should be. Telling it like it is will give you the most reliable feedback and make the test results accurate and useful.

# PERFORMANCE ZONE PROFILE

SCORING: 1 IS TOTAL DISAGREEMENT. C IS TOTAL AGREEMENT.

| | | |
|---|---|---|
| 1 | I can do anything I try. | 1 2 3 4 5 6 7 |
| 2 | I am constantly in over my head. | 1 2 3 4 5 6 7 |
| 3 | I'll try anything once. | 1 2 3 4 5 6 7 |
| 4 | I am an overachiever. | 1 2 3 4 5 6 7 |
| 5 | I don't like to try something I am unsure of. | 1 2 3 4 5 6 7 |
| 6 | I often get so involved that I lose track of time. | 1 2 3 4 5 6 7 |
| 7 | I'll do anything to achieve my goals. | 1 2 3 4 5 6 7 |
| 8 | I seek challenges. | 1 2 3 4 5 6 7 |
| 9 | I have a hard time pulling out of it when I fail. | 1 2 3 4 5 6 7 |
| 10 | I am cautious in my acceptance of new ideas. | 1 2 3 4 5 6 7 |
| 11 | My work is my life. | 1 2 3 4 5 6 7 |
| 12 | I am a stickler for details. | 1 2 3 4 5 6 7 |
| 13 | I play it safe. | 1 2 3 4 5 6 7 |
| 14 | I feel as if I have to constantly prove myself. | 1 2 3 4 5 6 7 |
| 15 | I want to be the best at what I do. | 1 2 3 4 5 6 7 |
| 16 | I'd rather be safe than sorry. | 1 2 3 4 5 6 7 |
| 17 | I don't spend enough time preparing for important events. | 1 2 3 4 5 6 7 |
| 18 | I'm a hard driver. | 1 2 3 4 5 6 7 |
| 19 | I have a dream. | 1 2 3 4 5 6 7 |
| 20 | I set my goals higher than I can reach. | 1 2 3 4 5 6 7 |
| 21 | I bite off more than I can chew. | 1 2 3 4 5 6 7 |
| 22 | I am an eternal optimist. | 1 2 3 4 5 6 7 |
| 23 | I don't like to take chances. | 1 2 3 4 5 6 7 |

| 24 | I think something through thoroughly before I act on it. | 1 2 3 4 5 6 7 |
|----|----|----|
| 25 | After failing at an important task, I feel that my life is not worth living. | 1 2 3 4 5 6 7 |
| 26 | I feel that I am always rushing. | 1 2 3 4 5 6 7 |
| 27 | I never give up. | 1 2 3 4 5 6 7 |
| 28 | I must do well. | 1 2 3 4 5 6 7 |
| 29 | I push myself to the limit. | 1 2 3 4 5 6 7 |
| 30 | My commitments leave me little time to relax. | 1 2 3 4 5 6 7 |
| 31 | I get high from work. | 1 2 3 4 5 6 7 |
| 32 | I play by the rules. | 1 2 3 4 5 6 7 |
| 33 | I carefully consider every possibility before making a move. | 1 2 3 4 5 6 7 |
| 34 | There is virtually nothing I can't do. | 1 2 3 4 5 6 7 |
| 35 | I tend to move on to the next thing before I finish what I am doing. | 1 2 3 4 5 6 7 |

## SCORING YOUR TEST

To score the Performance Zone Profile, you'll need a piece of paper. Set up six columns: Panic, Drone, C, CM, CF, and CT. These last three represent the Type C characteristics: commitment/passion (CM), confidence (CF) and control (CT).

Now, compare your answers from the test with those on the score sheet, which indicate the point value and performance zone for each possible answer (that is, a score of 2C = 2 points in the C column).

If your score on a question falls in the Panic (P) or Drone (D) category, simply add the point score to that column. If you score in the C Zone, give yourself the indicated number of points in the C column. Additionally, when you score a C, look at column no. D on the score sheet to determine the Type C characteristic tested by that question. (Some questions have only one characteristic; others, two.) Then, enter the number of C points you received for that answer into the appropriate Type C characteristic column. You get CM, CF, or CT points only when you have a C score.

For example, let's score question no. 1. If your answer was a 3, give yourself 1 point in the Drone column. If, on the other hand, your answer was a 5, give yourself 2 points in the C column and 2 points in both the CF and CT columns.

## INTERPRETING YOUR SCORE

Compare your total scores in the first three columns: Panic, Drone, and C. Your score will be highest in the zone you occupy the most often. This will indicate how you tend to stray from your C Zone. A Type C generally scores twice as many C points as Drone and Panic points combined.

The CM, CF, and CT columns will indicate which Type C characteristics are well developed and which need work. If your strength, in terms of these characteristics, far outweighs your weak points, you might be relying too much on that characteristic and too little on the others. A perfect Type C would score 30 points in each category. But who's perfect?

## RESULTS

The test results tell you how you saw yourself at the time you took it. Use this as a general guide to set your priorities for improvement. As you practice the techniques discussed in this book, your score will change. Taking the test every few months is a good way to review your development as a C.

# PERFORMANCE ZONE PROFILE

## *Score Sheet*

|    | 1  | 2  | 3  | 4  | 5  | 6  | 7  | 8     |
|----|----|----|----|----|----|----|----|-------|
| 1  | 2D | 2D | 1D | 2C | 2C | 1P | 3P | CF/CT |
| 2  | 2D | 1D | 1C | 2C | 1P | 2P | 3P | CM/CT |
| 3  | 2D | 2D | 1D | 2C | 2C | 1P | 3P | CF    |
| 4  | 3D | 2D | 1D | —  | 2C | 1P | 3P | CM    |
| 5  | 2P | 2C | 2C | 1D | 2D | 3D | 3P | CF/CT |
| 6  | 3D | 3D | 2D | 1D | 2C | 1C | 2P | CM    |
| 7  | 3D | 2D | 1D | 1C | 2C | 1P | 2P | CM    |
| 8  | 3D | 3D | 2D | 1D | 2C | 2C | 2P | CF/CT |
| 9  | —  | 2C | 1C | —  | —  | —  | —  | CF    |
| 10 | 2P | 1P | 2C | 1C | 1D | 2D | 3D | CF    |
| 11 | 3D | 2D | 1D | 1C | 2C | 1P | 3P | CM    |
| 12 | 3P | 2P | 1P | 2C | 1C | —  | 1D | CT    |
| 13 | 2P | 1C | 2C | —  | 1D | 2D | 3P | CF/CT |
| 14 | —  | —  | 1C | 2C | —  | —  | —  | CF    |
| 15 | 3D | 3D | 2D | 1D | 2C | 1C | 2P | CM    |
| 16 | 3P | 1P | 2C | —  | 1D | 2D | 3D | CF/CT |
| 17 | 1D | 2C | 1C | 1P | 2P | 3P | 3P | CT/CM |
| 18 | 3D | 2D | 1D | —  | 2C | 1P | 2P | CM    |
| 19 | 2D | 2D | 2D | 1D | 1C | 2C | 1P | CM    |
| 20 | 3D | 2D | 1D | —  | 2C | 1P | 3P | CM    |
| 21 | 3D | 2D | 1D | 1C | 2C | 1P | 3P | CM    |
| 22 | 3D | 2D | 1D | 1C | 2C | 1C | 2P | CF    |
| 23 | 2P | 2C | 2C | 1D | 2D | 3D | 3D | CF/CT |
| 24 | 3P | 3P | 1P | 1P | 2C | —  | 1D | CT    |
| 25 | 1C | 2C | 1C | —  | —  | —  | —  | CF    |
| 26 | 2D | 1D | 1C | 2C | 1P | 2P | 3P | CT    |
| 27 | 3D | 2D | 1D | 1C | 2C | 1P | 3P | CM    |
| 28 | —  | —  | 1C | 2C | —  | —  | —  | CF    |
| 29 | 3D | 3D | 2D | 1D | 2C | 1P | 3P | CM    |

| | | | | | | | | |
|---|---|---|---|---|---|---|---|---|
| **30** | 3D | 2D | 1D | 1C | 2C | 1P | 3P | CM/CT |
| **31** | 3D | 3D | 2D | 1D | — | 1C | 2C | CM |
| **32** | 2P | 4 | 2C | — | 1D | 1D | 3D | CF/CT |
| **33** | 3P | 2P | 1P | 1C | 2C | 1D | 2D | CT |
| **34** | 3D | 3D | 2D | 1D | 2C | 2C | 2P | CF |
| **35** | — | 1C | 2C | — | — | — | — | CT |

# 6

# OBSTACLES TO PEAK PERFORMANCE: THE VICIOUS CYCLE

## RIDING THE ROLLER COASTER

What stops us from being at our best more often? Why does our performance seem to peak and plummet with such maddening unpredictability? Why can we hit a great drive on one hole and duff the next? How can you go from a breakthrough to a breakdown run on the slopes in just a few minute? Why are we able to meet deadlines with ease, surpass quotas, and transform potential problems into great opportunities at certain times, while at others, we choke in meetings, find it impossible to get overdue reports finished, or feel that sales are harder to come by than snow in the

Sahara? How is it that we can go from the Peak Zone to the Panic or Drone Zone so quickly?

## PERFORMANCE TRIGGERS

One of the first things we ask the participants in a seminar is to list the types of situations they believe cause them to end up in the Panic Zone or the Drone Zone. The following is a sampling of their responses:

| | |
|---|---|
| deadlines | speaking in front of large groups |
| quotas | meetings with senior personnel |
| changes | new information |
| budget cuts and reviews | new clients |
| tight economy | money |
| competition | Monday morning |
| new boss | machines breaking down |
| problems at home | shortage of staff |
| traffic jams | parking |
| too many e-mails | asking for a raise |

This list is based on the assumption that the *situation* causes us to end up in the Panic Zone or the Drone Zone. Take, for example, one situation that seems high on most people's list: speaking to large groups.

"Has this situation ever not been a problem? Have you ever given a good talk?" we asked William T., the program director of a historic resort and conference center, who gives the introductory talk to business groups that come to the facility. "Sure," he said, "sometimes, when I'm relaxed and confident, I tell jokes and get to know the people in the group. When I'm like that, the talk goes great, it's fun, and I make everybody feel at home.

"Unfortunately, that's not usually the case," he continued, "Often, when I get up to speak, I have this little voice in my head that says, 'They're tired from their trip and didn't come here to listen to my spiel about the history of the place and that the fabulous stones for the building had to be carried over the mountain by horse and buggy. They just want to check in or hit the bar and aren't interested in when the restaurants are open and how to make tee times.' When I'm feeling like that, I try too hard to be funny, and I'm flat and bomb."

When William thinks the audience isn't interested, he becomes nervous and performs poorly. When he doesn't feel that way, he does fine and even has fun. Obviously, the talks don't propel William into his Panic Zone. It's his *attitude* about them.

## IT'S NOT THE ECONOMY

This isn't to say that a situation such as the current economic crisis doesn't influence your thinking and actions. Ultimately, it's your attitude to the crisis that determines how you will respond.

We recently conducted a program for sales people in a management training business that was having a tough time in this tight economy. It is informative to see how two of these group responded to these tough times.

Louis A. was in the biggest slump of his career. "Everybody's cut their budget for training and a lot of the programs I sold are being canceled. There's just no money around. The way

I'm being avoided, I feel like I am peddling a communicable disease. It's gotten to the point that I'm not even making calls. What's the use?"

Charlene M., on the other hand, had gone 25 percent over quota for the previous quarter. "Sure, the economy is tight, and budgets for our programs are being cut, but some people are still buying. I've just got to work harder to find them. Actually, the economy has helped me in one way. There's less competition because many of our competitors have gone belly up or have laid people off. So, when I do find someone who is interested, I usually get the order. I've actually opened quite a few new accounts."

Same circumstance, opposite responses. The economy didn't cause Louis to do poorly and Charlene to do well. Their responses did. Louis's defeatist attitude caused him to nosedive into the Drone Zone. Charlene's optimism and confidence about the same situation enabled her to perform at peak levels. Whereas Louis saw the economy as an obstacle, Charlene saw it as an opportunity.

*Situations and tasks are neutral. The individual's attitude toward them determines what zone he will play in and how effective he will be.* Top performers don't allow circumstances to dictate their performance. They realize that situations do have an effect, but that ultimately, their attitude about them makes the difference. "Sure, we have a bad economy and interest rates are high—that's the environment we are in," Charles A. Lynch, the former CEO of HDL Corporation told me. "But now's the time to be stronger, to take advantage of the situation. Now's the time to get a jump on the competition by being first and fastest out of the box. Sure, there's less business out there, but if I'm aggressive I'm going to get it. Then, when the economy comes back, I'm going to be ahead of the competition."

## YOU SEE WHAT YOU BELIEVE

Many people believe that their attitude is caused by what they see; that your anxiety, as you stand up to speak in a meeting, is caused by seeing the size of the group This definitely happens, but more often, you probably started feeling anxious when you first knew you were going to speak in that meeting, and the anxiety escalated dramatically while you were waiting to go on. So, you were already in your Panic Zone by the time you got up to present.

Sure, you probably felt scared when you looked down and saw the steepness and size of the bumps on the ski slope you were about to takBut just as likely, you were already feeling anxious before you even got to the top of the lift. So, by the time you got to the top of the run, your heart was already pounding, and you were ready to hit the lodge.

## PROJECTION

*What you see is most often not what is before your eyes but what's projected by your attitude.* In psychology, this phenomenon is called *projection*. Projecting your attitude onto a situation is like putting a colored filter over your camera lens.

That filter colors everything you see. Your attitude colors your perception of a situation just as the filter does. Doubt and anxiety cause you to see the situation through a "screen of fear." Your apprehension clouds everything, and everything appears more intimidating and threatening than it really is. Ski slopes look frighteningly steep, and the audience to whom you are speaking looks as if it is made up of the Wicked Witch of the West and Godzilla in a three-piece suit.

Hall of Fame Baseball player Mike Schmidt says that when you are in a slump and worried about it, all you see are obstacles on the field that will prevent your ball from dropping in for a hit. Even the second-base umpire appears to be wearing a glove at these times.[1]

## THE NEGATIVE MAGNET

*Your attitude not only colors your perception of a situation; it seeks out that which will reinforce it.* When feeling anxious standing on top of a ski slope, your eyes are drawn to what scares you—the big moguls and bare patches. Similarly, when anxious about the presentation you are giving, your eyes are naturally drawn to the person in the audience who reinforces your anxiety—the guy looking at his watch, the person yawning, the woman with arms folded across her chest. Focusing on that which reinforces your anxiety and stress causes you to become even more anxious and stressed.

# THE VICIOUS CYCLE

Underscoring this relationship of attitude to performance, tennis great Billie Jean King says, "If you believe you will fail, you will find some way to fail."[2] Coming at it from the opposite end, Tom Landry, former coach of the Dallas Cowboys, who during his tenure were the winningest team in the National Football League, said, "However you think determines how you play."[3]

A negative attitude not only colors your immediate perception and causes you to seek out confirmation by focusing on that which scares you; it also has an insidious effect on your physical responses and your behavior. It then winds into other areas of your life, becoming a vicious cycle that affects everything you do.

The following incident illustrates this vicious cycle effect. Susan E., in her early thirties, was a single mother of two children. When her children started school, she went to graduate school for her M.B.A. After earning her degree, she got a job as an assistant product manager for a consumer product goods company. Within five years, she was the director of new product development and had been responsible for two very successful product introductions. Although she was highly regarded in the company, and liked her work, Susan felt underpaid and was having difficulty making ends meet. When the company announced a wage freeze, she decided to look for a higher-paying job.

Her first interview was for a group product management job in the same field, one for which she knew she was extremely well qualified. Although her recommendations and track record were outstanding, her attitude didn't reflect her experience. She felt that she didn't come across well in interviews and worried that her M.B.A., a requirement for this job, wasn't from a name school.

Describing how she felt as she sat waiting in the reception room to be interviewed, Susan said, "My heart was pounding; my palms were sweating. I felt like I was fourteen and about to go on my first date. I couldn't concentrate on the magazine I was reading. A man and a woman were also waiting to be interviewed, and I couldn't take my eyes off them. They both looked confident, relaxed, and seemed so professional, which made me even more nervous. Suddenly, I was only aware of how frumpy I looked. My palms were sweating; my hair wasn't right, and my attaché case looked like it came from a discount store. I even noticed a spot on my suit."

When her name was called, Susan said her knees "felt like water." The interviewer appeared to frown when she came into his office, which increased her stress level. She smiled feebly as she sat down and "When he asked me questions, my mind seemed like a jumble, and I began to talk too fast and say too much. There was so much that I wanted to tell him about what I was doing, but it kept coming out wrong. Then, I'd have to correct myself. When he looked at the clock on his desk, my heart sank. I was sure he was in a hurry, and I wanted to make certain I told him everything, so I continued to rush through more of my qualifications."

Afterward, Susan realized that she had neglected to

mention several accomplishments relevant to the job. She felt that she had done terribly in the interview and was depressed, as she headed back to her office. The rejection letter she received three days later confirmed her original belief that she wasn't good at interviewing.

The vicious cycle diagram below illustrates how your attitude dictates how you perceive a situation and how you respond and perform. Susan's belief that she wouldn't do well made her tense and nervous before she even got to the interview. The projection of her fear and lack of confidence onto the situation made the interview seem very threatening and the interviewer seem intimidating and uninterested. It also made the other people waiting in the reception area seem more confident and much more professional than she did. This made her even tenser and resulted in her flubbing the interview. Susan's lack of confidence in this situation caused her to lose control of herself and perform poorly. Her Panic Zone performance reinforced her lack of confidence about interviewing, which would make it that much harder for her to do well in subsequent interviews.

## POOR PERFORMANCE TO LOW SELF-ESTEEM: THE RIPPLE EFFECT

Like ripples when you throw a rock into a pond, once a vicious cycle is established, it begins to affect everything you do. When Susan got back to her office after the interview, she was in a foul mood and lost her temper at her secretary over a small error. In a brainstorming meeting for new prod-

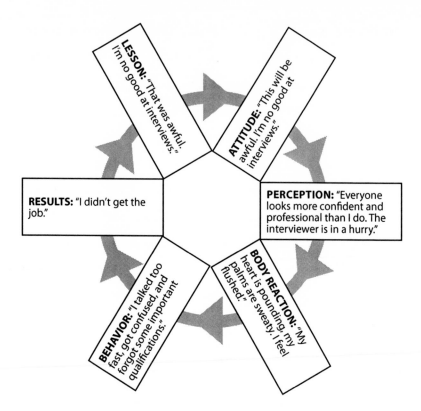

**LESSON:** "That was awful! I'm no good at interviews."

**ATTITUDE:** "This will be awful. I'm no good at interviews."

**RESULTS:** "I didn't get the job."

**PERCEPTION:** "Everyone looks more confident and professional than I do. The interviewer is in a hurry."

**BEHAVIOR:** "I talked too fast, got confused, and forgot some important qualifications."

**BODY REACTION:** "My heart is pounding, my palms are sweaty, I feel flushed."

ucts, at which she usually performed well, providing energy and creative spark, Susan was very tentative and unfocused. "I couldn't get my mind off that damn interview."

Later that day, at a monthly progress review with senior management, she was halfhearted in her recommendations and responses to their questions. As she left the meeting, she noticed several of the managers glancing at each other in disappointment.

Arriving home that evening, Susan found a mess in the kitchen, not an uncommon occurrence in a home with two pre-teen children. But this night, she lost her temper and yelled at her kids, something she rarely did. "I began to wonder if I was even good at being a mother, or anything else, for that matter." She was now thoroughly depressed.

An attitude of failure not only causes you to do poorly in one situation but also can cause you to plummet into a slump affecting every aspect of your life. By the end of the day, Susan's original attitude of "I'm not good at interviewing" had turned into "I'm not much good at anything." Her lack of confidence regarding one specific situation had transferred into a lack of confidence about herself.

This progression from poor performance to poor self-image is like a whirlpool. The deeper you get into it, the faster it spins, pulling you down and making it more difficult to get out. Your Peak Zone, from the bottom of the whirlpool, seems totally out of reach. The whirlpool effect looks like this:

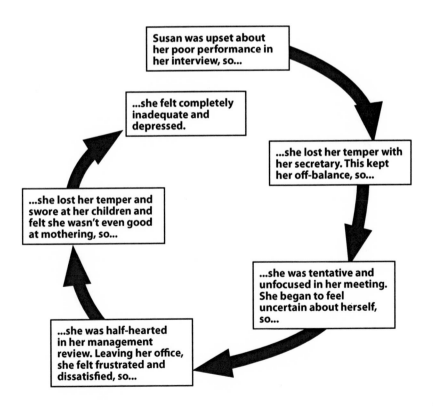

## Vicious Cycle

Think of a situation that you usually get anxious about and often perform poorly, and answer the following questions at the appropriate places on the diagram. (p. 40)

1. Situation. . .
2. Attitude—when confronted with this situation.
3. Perception—how the situation appears to me; how I perceive it.
4. Body—my physical response to the situation; what I feel.
5. Behavior—how I perform in this situation; what I do.
6. Results—how things turn out; how I do.
7. Lesson—what I learn from this situation.

## The Vital Cycle: The Peak Zone

In one of my seminars, I asked the members of a top college basketball team to imagine they were on the foul line in the last seconds of a championship game; their team was down by one point. If they made both points, they would win. If not . . .

"What is going on in your mind as you stand there waiting to shoot?" I asked.

"I'm thinking about what would happen if I missed." "I've got to sink both shots." one responded.

"I'll never be able to look my friends in the eye if I blow these shots." another said. "A blur" someone else said.

But the teams high scorer, a big forward, who I later learned was an honorable-mention All-American, said, "Hey, I wouldn't be thinking about any of those things. That just messes me up. I love those tight spots. They're my chance to get some good ink, to be a hero. Hell, I've made ninety-five out of a hundred foul shots in practice. Sinking that shot is a snap! I concentrate on the back of the rim, just like I do in practice. Just me and the basket. I don't even hear the crowd. The basket even begins to look bigger." Then, he took a deep breath, exhaled slowly, faked a shot, and laughed. "Right in."

This athlete's attitude, based on his experience, helped him perceive the situation optimistically, which enabled him to concentrate more intensely and perform at his best. He created a vital cycle for himself.

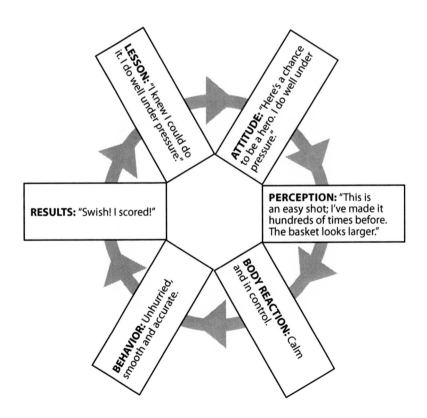

LESSON: "I knew I could do it. I do well under pressure."

ATTITUDE: "Here's a chance to be a hero. I do well under pressure."

RESULTS: "Swish! I scored!"

PERCEPTION: "This is an easy shot; I've made it hundreds of times before. The basket looks larger."

BEHAVIOR: Unhurried, smooth and accurate.

BODY REACTION: Calm and in control.

# THE RIPPLE EFFECT: ONE VITAL CYCLE LEADS TO ANOTHER

Vital cycles, like vicious ones, constantly expand like ripples in a lake into which a stone has been thrown. Imagine the effect on the rest of Susan's day and evening if she had had a more positive attitude about herself in that interview, the way she normally had in her job. It would have carried over into her brainstorming session, into the meeting with senior management, and with her children at home.

## *Vital Cycle*

Think of a situation where you perform in your Peak Zone. Fill out the questions below in the appropriate places on the diagram.

1. Situation. . .
2. Attitude—when confronted with this situation.
3. Perception—how the situation appears to me; how I perceive it.
4. Body—my physical response to the situation; what I feel.
5. Behavior—how I perform in this situation; what I do.
6. Results—how things turn out; how I do.
7. Lesson—what I learn from this situation.

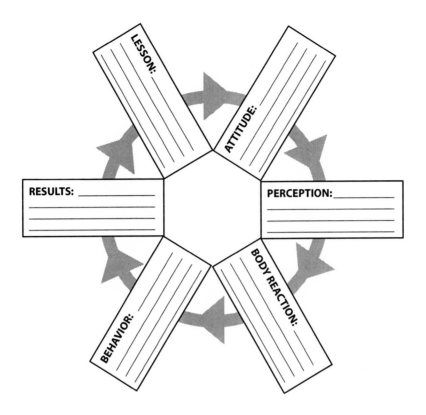

RESULTS: _____
_____
_____

PERCEPTION:_____
_____
_____

LESSON:

ATTITUDE:

BEHAVIOR:

BODY REACTION:

## TRANSFORMING VICIOUS CYCLES TO VITAL CYCLES

Vicious cycles can be broken and vital ones begun by increasing your confidence, commitment, or control. The techniques for developing these characteristics are simple, easy to implement, and most important, they work. You can use them as many peak performers do when preparing for an important event. You can also use these techniques during pressure situations to decrease stress, concentrate better, express yourself more clearly, and be calm and sure under fire.

Each technique discussed later throughout the book will help you develop a specific characteristic. Just as one vital cycle leads to another, increasing your strength in one characteristic strengthens the others as well. Increasing your confidence, therefore, will lead to increased self-control and a deeper commitment and vice versa. You can't lose. Any technique described in the following chapters can lead you into your Peak Zone.

First, it's important to learn to recognize and overcome some main mental obstacles that get you into the Panic or Drone Zones.

# 7

# COLD FEET, DRY MOUTH, POUNDING HEART—NERVOUS IS NORMAL

Speaking in public is one of the highest-pressure situations for most people, even those you'd never suspect. Jerry Seinfeld used to joke that, at funerals, most people would rather be the person *in* the casket than the one giving the eulogy. Stefan Hofmann, director of Boston University's Center for Anxiety and Related Disorders says that dread of public speaking is the most common human fear.[1]

## NERVOUS IS NATURAL

It's natural to be nervous, anxious, or even petrified before an important presentation or any high-pressure situation, especially when there's a lot riding on the outcome. You might think that "tough guys" don't get scared. Bogey didn't; Arnold doesn't. Bruce Willis scared? Are you kidding? Never happens. Not true!

Before a pressure situation, even heavy hitters feel anxious. Former British Prime Minister Winston Churchill, one of the most adept ever in the bulldog-tough ring of Britain's Parliament, used to say that he felt as though a block of ice was in his stomach every time he got up to speak there. Activist Gloria Steinem, a major spokesperson in the fight for women's rights and a founder of *Ms. Magazine,* said, "the very idea of speaking to a group, much less before a big audience, was enough to make my heart pound and my mouth go dry."[2] And Luciano Pavarotti, one of the opera's all-time greatest stars said, "We go onstage with the same feeling every night—'I'm afraid.' And if someone says they're not afraid, they are a liar."[3]

You'd think that experienced stage actors would have overcome their fears. Sir Laurence Olivier, one of the greatest to ever "hit the boards," contemplated retiring from the theater because of stage fright. "It is always waiting outside the door," he said. Of his famous performance in *Othello,* Olivier wrote, "I had to beg my Iago, Frank Finlay, not to leave the stage when I had a soliloquy, but to stay in the wings downstage where I could see him, since I feared I might not be able to stay there in front of the audience by myself."[4] And that's not from some high schooler in his first play, that's from *Olivier.* Even the great Barbra Streisand suffers from chronic stage fright.[5]

Describing his stage fright doing stand-up, Academy Award winning actor Jamie Foxx says, "Oh, man, that's horrendous."[6] And Golden Globe winner, actor Hugh Grant, an Oxford graduate, and the star of many movies, including *Four Weddings and a Funeral, Notting Hill*, and *Bridget Jones' Diary*, which have grossed more than $2.5b, said of his last few films, "I had terrible stage fright. I would do the scenes in rehearsal, and it would be fine. But then, suddenly, you feel tight and you panic, and get really, really tight, and you can't remember your lines."[7]

Think the great athletes don't feel fear before a pressure game? Think again. NBA Hall-of-Famer Bill Russell used to throw up before most games. Edwin Moses, former world record holder in the grueling 400 meter hurdles, who won more than 100 races in a row and four Olympic gold medals, said that each time he raced, it felt as if he was being led to his execution.[8]

Swimming world record holder Katie Hoff had to be rescued and pulled out of the pool because of a panic attack while a teenager. US Olympic coach Mark Schubert was quoted as saying that the anxiety that made her palms clammy, her heart race, and her mind a tangled web was a well-known opponent on the world scene.[9]

Even the Tiger feels it. Describing an incident on the first tee in a tournament, Woods said, "I teed up my golf ball... and thought *I'm fine, no big deal, I can do this.* I took the club back and, I swear, it felt like it took about 15 seconds for the club to get to the top of my swing. It was so heavy. I have never experienced anything like that in my life."[10]

# NERVOUS IS NORMAL

The bottom line is that no matter how experienced you are, you're not normal if you're not stressed before a pressure situation. A good example of that is Sean Brawley, a former college all-American tennis player at USC who now conducts corporate leadership programs internationally. Brawley, who is obviously not new to pressure situations, says; "I've given hundreds of workshops, and yet, before I start a program, I still get panicked. In fact, sometimes, I've gotten a panic attack where I actually can't talk for a few minutes.[11]

I've given more than 1,800 keynote speeches at major conferences, and you'd think I'd be cool before going on. Not so, I still feel that pre-performance anxiety. So, no matter how experienced you are, *nervous is normal* before a pressure situation.

# FEAR AS AN ALLY

There's an up side to all that nervousness—without the fear, you probably won't perform well. If you're not at least a little on edge at these times, you'll most likely be too relaxed, over-confident, and lack the energy and adrenaline boost that fear provides.

Fear can act as an incredibly positive force, providing the energy and focus for you to soar beyond your expectations. Former Coca Cola President Don Keough, a very motivating and inspiring speaker, said, "Everyone experiences a certain amount of anxiety (before a speech). The adrenaline is flowing, and you can feel your blood pressure bouncing and your heart pounding. But," he added, "you can learn that it can be a positive force rather than a negative one."[12]

## KNOWING YOUR ADVERSARY

One reason that fear can be so insidious and potent is that it is self-fulfilling as well as self-reinforcing, often *causing* the very thing you're afraid will happen. And once triggered, it gathers momentum like a wildfire after a drought.

Awareness of how *fear* works is the secret to controlling it and using its powerful energy as an ally. Each link in fear's vicious cycle, as you will see in later chapters, actually provides the solution for overcoming its symptoms. Just as in any competition, the better you know your adversary, the easier it is to counter its moves. Therefore, the sooner you recognize the signs of fear, the easier it will be to turn this vicious cycle into a vital one and perform in that Peak Zone more often.

## EVERYTHING'S A BEAR

Fear distorts your perception, making situations look more dangerous and difficult than they really are, while your ability to handle them appears diminished. And what might happen IF . . . is too awful to even think about.

Many years ago, I was backpacking with a group of people in the Sierras. In the evening, we were told to hang our food high in a tree so that bears wouldn't steal it. Being new to the

West, I had never seen a bear outside a zoo. But I had heard horror stories about how big, strong, and fast they were, how they could rip open locked car doors with their claws, and how they had mutilated people in their sleeping bags while foraging for their food. After hearing about a few of these incidents, I was afraid that the food the bears would find would be me.

When it came time to go to sleep, I was petrified. I put my sleeping bag down near the fire in the middle of the group. It didn't matter that the ground there was full of rocks. I figured it was the last place the bears would hit. As I lay there with my heart pounding, sleep was impossible. Every sound was a bear. Someone rolling over was a bear moving. The wind blowing through the trees was a bear sneaking up on me. When the moon created shadows through the trees, it was a bear right there next to me.

Usually, the problem isn't ferocious bears. But critical clients or tight deadlines are no different; your mind plays tricks on you when you are afraid. Remote improbabilities seem realistic possibilities.

## THE TELESCOPE EFFECT

Fear causes your imagination to run wild. Everything seems more difficult and dangerous than it is. Cus D'Amato, the legendary fight manager, talked about how young fighters entering the ring for the first time usually scare themselves into losing. "The young fighter always perceives his first-time opponent as being bigger, stronger, and faster than he is,[13]" says

D'Amato. I used to have that same feeling when I was a young competitive swimmer. As I'd stand on the starting block, I would look at my competition, thinking about how big and long his arms were and that he'd definitely outstroke me.

When we are anxious and stressed on the job, we distort reality in the same way. Situations seem much more difficult and more important than they really are. You walk into your office worried about meeting a deadline, and the pile of papers on your desk seems mountainous and the e-mail list seems never ending. You feel as if the presentation you have to give, the report you must submit, or the sale you have to make involves life-or-death consequences.

At times such as this, as in any vicious cycle, we tend to notice only those things that reinforce and increase our fear. A frightened skier only sees huge moguls and ice and doesn't observe that most of the slope is easy. A fear-filled speaker only notices the person in the audience yawning and looking at his watch and doesn't realize that everyone else is listening intently.

Fear causes you to perceive a situation as if you were alternately looking through each end of a telescope. The difficulty or importance of the task is greatly magnified as you look through one end. Your ability to perform is minimized as you look through the other. These distorted views reinforce your fear, which blocks confidence, douses your fire, and prevents you from operating in the Peak Zone.

The following diagram shows how each link in the vicious cycle works, which will help you to recognize and overcome it more quickly and easily.

# THE FEAR CYCLE

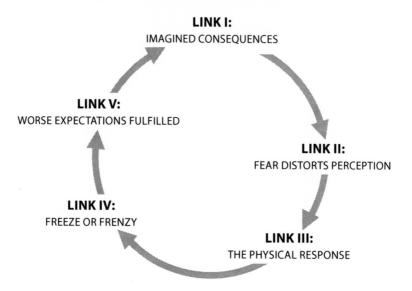

**LINK I:**
IMAGINED CONSEQUENCES

**LINK V:**
WORSE EXPECTATIONS FULFILLED

**LINK II:**
FEAR DISTORTS PERCEPTION

**LINK IV:**
FREEZE OR FRENZY

**LINK III:**
THE PHYSICAL RESPONSE

## *1: The Doomsday Scenario—Imagined Consequences*

Fear also causes us to jump to worst-case conclusions. When I asked the marketing director of a major health insurance company what he thought of President Obama's proposed government health insurance option, he responded. "It's awful! It'll put the insurance business out of business. And if that happens, I am out of a job, and I don't know where I would get another one. It's really tough out there with so much unemployment. And I've got kids in school, a big mortgage, and car payments." And it sounded as if the next step for him was sitting on a curb drinking Ripple out of a paper bag. So, in effect, he jumped from a question about a proposed government program to the food line in about 10 seconds. That's what fear does; it jolts us by causing us to jump to worst-case scenario.

Sandy B., a real estate agent and mother of two young daughters, was elected spokesperson for the neighborhood committee that had been organized to prevent a large chain from opening a store in their area. Waiting to give her testimony to the Board of Supervisors, she was petrified. "I'm so nervous, I can hardly breathe. I've only got five minutes to present our case, and I'm worried I'm going to forget something. And if I don't know the answer to one of their questions, we'll never get this measure approved. If I blow this, it's going to ruin my reputation in the neighborhood. My friends are going to think I'm stupid, and I'll never get another listing for my business. Why did I ever volunteer for this in the first place?"

Fear causes the imagination to make challenging situations seem like impending doom. The consequences of bombing in a speech seem catastrophic, as we imagine the worst happening. It's common for people, before a presentation, to imagine their minds will go blank, and they'll look stupid or worse. Speakers fear that they'll bore the audience, people will walk out in the middle, and they'll never get another job.

## "...Or Else"

Fear magnifies the consequences of failing to horrible and catastrophic dimensions. Doomsday lurks beyond the meeting for which you're late, the sale you might not make, and the deadline you might miss. It's not just the fear that your speech or presentation won't go well and that you won't get the result you had hoped for; suddenly, it's your job, your reputation, your self-worth that's on the line.

"I was afraid of failure," said Hall-of-Fame baseball player Mike Schmidt. "I'd go up and squeeze the bat and say, 'I've got to get a hit.'"[14] But "Gotta" is really only half a thought. The other half is the "or else"—the consequences you fear if you fail to do what you think you've "gotta."

The consequences Schmidt feared if he didn't get a hit were "50,000 people will boo me," or "I'll lose that contract."[15] The fear that exaggerates the difficulty of a situation also exaggerates the imagined consequences. You *act* as if any fall on the ski slope will result in a broken leg or the consequences of losing a sale will be losing your job, causing you to freeze or go into a frenzy.

That's what fear does when unchecked. It takes a simple situation and makes it do or die, and mostly die.

## 2: FEAR DISTORTS PERCEPTION— YOU SEE WHAT YOU BELIEVE

When we lived in Venice Beach, California, my wife and I would go to the beach at sunset, wearing rose-colored sunglasses, which heightened the colors and made everything look even brighter and more beautiful. Fear does the opposite. When you're scared, it's like putting on a pair of gray gloom glasses that make everything seem scarier and more intimidating than it actually is.

To the nervous golfer preparing to putt, the cup seems the size of a dime. To the scared skier, the intermediate slope looks like the face of El Capitan in Yosemite (sheer!). To nervous presenters, the audience seems to be made up of opening-night critics waiting to pounce. Rather than some perfectly innocent managers in the front row, we see Darth Vader in a coat and tie, the Joker, and that old Wicked Witch.

Making matters worse is that unchecked, your eyes will always be drawn to what heightens your anxiety and stress level—the sand trap on the golf course, the huge mogul on the ski slope. As many presenters know, your gaze at these times seems glued to the person you need to avoid looking at—the woman yawning or the man checking his Blackberry. Once a guy in the audience at one of my speeches was reading the newspaper, and I couldn't take my eyes off him. In that room full of 900 people, he was the only person I was focusing on.

This distorted perception of reality that makes everything seem worse and scarier than it really is, catapults your fear to an even higher level— which, of course, makes everything seem even more worse and scarier. And the cycle continues.

## 3: THUMP, THUMP, YOU FEEL WHAT YOU SEE

Fear sneaks up on us. We often don't realize the extent to which it affects our perceptions and performance, but our physical response often provides the first sign that we're caught in a vicious cycle.

- Your heart is pounding so hard that you're sure everyone can hear it.
- Your palms and pits are sweating.
- Your stomach has the butterflies, and they're fluttering out of control.

- You can't seem to breathe or catch your breath.
- You feel tired or seem to have no energy.
- You feel like you're having caffeine rush  with way  too  much energy, and your mind is darting from one thing to another, preventing you from concentrating on anything.
- Your mouth feels like the sands of the Sahara.
- Your throat is tight, causing your voice to be three octaves higher than normal.

## 4: FREEZE OR FRENZY: YOU PERFORM HOW YOU FEEL

Fear that has reached a crescendo causes one of two basic responses. We either freeze up—our minds going blank, important points nowhere to be found, our voices repeating "uh..." as our mouths open and close like errant flycatchers—or the opposite—the mind darts like a hyperactive hummingbird, our gaze flitting from one person to another. In this wired, fast-forward state, we talk too fast, race from point to point without stopping, and don't listen to comments or make eye contact with the  audience.

## 5: YOUR WORST EXPECTATIONS ARE REALIZED

The result of either freeze or frenzy is that we perform far below our ability or knowledge level, and the group doesn't buy what we're selling—whether it's our product, our message, or ourselves. Fear has caused our performance to match our direst expectations—our prophecy has become self-fulfilling. Notice that this has *nothing* to do with our ability to present or the knowledge we're trying to impart. It's that fear has sabotaged our efforts.

## And Next Time

We learn from every experience and tend to remember our crashes much more vividly than our successes. For example, if you gave three great responses to questions from your audience and fumbled one, which will you remember most clearly after that meeting? If you're like most people, you'll remember the one you blew—not to see what went wrong and fix it for next time, but to torture yourself for being unprepared and inept. This response will deflate your confidence and cause you to panic the next time you're asked to give a presentation. That's exactly what happened to me after the horrific presentation to Procter and Gamble when I shuffled my carefully prepared index cards.

The result is that the vicious cycle is reinforced. Only now, it's a little more deeply etched in our minds. And if that's not bad enough, the effects of this poor experience are pervasive, influencing not only future performances, but our mood and self-confidence as well.

Below is the diagram of a fear cycle for a young manager making her first presentation at a conference of her company's top executives.

As you can see, fear's vicious cycle is truly insidious, feeding

**LINK I:**
IMAGINED CONSEQUENCES
"I'm going to look bad"
"I won't be able to answer all the questions"
"I'm going to lose my job"

**LINK V:**
WORST EXPECTATIONS FULFILLED
"I was right, they don't trust me"
"I knew I'd blow it"

**LINK II:**
FEAR DISTORTS PERCEPTION
Audience looks like opening night critics

**LINK IV:**
FREEZE OR FRENZY
Talks too fast
Forgets key points
Stumbles, mumbles, bumbles

**LINK III:**
THE PHYSICAL RESPONSE
Clamped Jaw • Overheated

on itself and becoming self-fulfilling, self-perpetuating, and self-reinforcing. The *good news* is that once you become aware of its signs and signals, you can break the cycle at any link in its chain.

Take a moment now and apply the diagram to one of your own experiences, one in which the vicious cycle applies or has applied in your life. Then, fill in each link in the cycle. The next few chapters will give you tools and strategies to help break out of that pattern and prevent you from getting caught in it again.

Learning to control the energy of fear will transform a vicious cycle into a vital one, enabling you to perform far better than you've ever imagined and to get into the Peak Zone—by choice, not chance—more often and for longer periods.

# 8

# CONQUERING FEAR—INCREASING CONFIDENCE

## FEAR ZAPS CONFIDENCE

It's no news that confidence is critical for peak performance and success and key to starting vital cycles and operating in your Peak Zone. But the confidence that keeps you in your Peak Zone is not just confidence in your ability to perform. Ultimately, it is confidence in yourself, an experience of your own self-worth, that radiates out into everything you do.

The obstacle that most often inhibits confidence, whether it is about your ability to excel in a specific situation or about your belief in yourself, is fear. Fear drives you out of the Peak Zone and into either a Panic Zone frenzy or a Drone Zone freeze. The way you handle this threat to your confidence will determine the zone in which you perform.

"You can't be a winner and be afraid to lose," said SAGA Corporation's former chairman and CEO Charles Lynch. "It's antithetical to success. Fear will prevent you from feeling confident enough to call on those big clients and play in the big leagues."

## FEAR OF FAILING

Peter J. is vice president and creative director for one of the world's largest advertising agencies. His income is well into six figures, and he has won many awards for his TV commercials. He has an apartment in the city, a house in the country, and two children in college. Everyone who knows Peter says, "He has it made." Everyone, except Peter.

"I originally got into the ad business as a way to make some money while I became a writer. Well, here I am at forty-five, and I haven't written a thing. I have an idea for a great screenplay, but I never start working on it. I'm afraid it's not going to be good enough, so, I continue working on these ads, even though my heart's not in it."

Dr. Rachel D. the head nutritionist for a large breakfast cereal manufacturer is well known in her field and frequently called upon to speak at major conferences, write articles for professional journals, and advise on new products. Her phone is always ringing, and someone is always popping into her office for advice and help on their projects or personal diets.

Rachel's problem is setting limits. "I make myself endlessly available because I'm afraid that if I turn down a request to write an article or speak at a conference, I won't be asked again, which would limit my effectiveness and visibility.

"To make matters worse, I'm afraid to even close my office door because word will get out that I've become highfalutin and inaccessible which would alienate my colleagues. So I say yes to everything and everyone. As result I'm constantly in over my head and don't have time to get my own work done. All I do is run around taking care of everybody else."

Peter's fear of failing to meet an imaginary standard robs him of the confidence needed to challenge himself and take the risk to write his screenplay. Therefore, despite his many accomplishments, he remains in his Drone Zone, frustrated and disappointed, , but still unwilling to leave his safe place.

Rachel's fear of losing contacts in the industry and alienating her colleagues prevents her from saying no when she needs to. Because she tries to do too much, she ends up over her head and out of control and in her Panic Zone.

## FEAR OF FAILING AND LOSING

The main fear that most of us face is the fear of losing or failing and its consequences. Top performers, though they hate to fail, aren't *afraid* to. "Losing is a part of winning," Dick Munroe, the former chief executive officer of Time Inc., told me. "It's like playing tennis. You're always going to lose a few points, a couple of games, and even some sets. If you don't, you're not challenging yourself. If you're afraid of losing, you'll hold back. You don't hit winners that way. The same is true in any area of life. If you're afraid to fail, you'll lack the confidence needed to go all out and give it everything you've got. If you are afraid to lose, you'll never win." Sounds like a Catch-22? It is.

Peak performers know that, in this rapidly changing time, they have to be innovative, to take risks, to confront the many challenges set forth by this new age. They also know that, with risk, come mistakes and failures. Fletcher Byrom the former CEO of the Koppers Company, has a Ninth Commandment— Make sure you generate a reasonable number of mistakes.[1] *Mistakes or failures aren't obstacles to confidence. The fear of them is.*

## FABULOUS FAILURES

We all know that people such as Lincoln, Edison, and the Wright brothers had a number of major failures and made innumerable mistakes before finally achieving the successes for which they are remembered. In any walk of life, in any era, those who have succeeded are usually those who have learned from their mistakes, persevered, and gone to levels of excellence because of what they learned along the way. I once read that the average multimillionaire entrepreneur has gone bankrupt 3.75 times. Walter Wriston, the former chairman of Citibank and who, at the time, was the most revered person in the financial world, said, "Failure isn't a crime; failure to learn from failure, that's the crime." Below are some examples of little known failures that led to major successes.

- When UCLA's legendary basketball coach John Wooden first introduced the fast break to basketball, his team committed the highest number of turnovers and fouls in memory. But Wooden knew mistakes were part of learning and went on to perfect this new offense and win 10 national championships in 12 years, one of the most remarkable achievements in sports history.

- Sports Illustrated's success was a long time in the making, having lost money for the first 10 years.

- Just out of college, Phillip Moffit, along with four other partners, started Campus Voice, a magazine that served as a campus guide for a college's activities. Realizing a small profit on the first edition, they decided to branch out and published 20 editions, and lost $100,000. Thinking they had the right formula but needing to increase volume, they then published editions for 60 colleges and lost $300,000. Still not deterred, they continued expanding and published 100 editions and lost half a million dollars. And Moffitt was still only in his mid-twenties.

  "Failure is always a part of success," Moffitt told me. Learning from these failures, he and his group went on to several very successful ventures in publishing. Eventually, with partner Chris Whittle, he bought Esquire Magazine when it was in a tailspin, turned it around, and sold it to Hearst.

- New York City Mayor Michael Bloomberg founded the phenomenally successful Bloomberg L.P., which made him one of the country's richest men with a net worth of $16b. He says it all started with his having been demoted and placed in charge of Salomon Brothers' IT division, which was thought to be beneath the attention of most senior partners. Two years later, he was fired from Salomon, which he views as "the best thing that ever happened to [him]"[2] and eventually went on to found the firm that made him his fortune.

- Tom Landry, Bill Walsh, and Chuck Knoll accounted for nine of the Super Bowl victories from 1974–89. What else do they have in common? They had the worst records of first season head coaches in NFL history.

Although I wouldn't put myself in the class of these people, my speaking and writing careers have been quite successful. Prior to that, however, I had three entrepreneurial failure notches in my belt, and had been fired from two other jobs.

## FEAR'S WARNING SIGNALS

An insidious aspect of fear is that you are often not conscious of what you are afraid of. Yet, your heart pounds so loudly, it feels as if it were going to burst out of your chest; your thoughts are bouncing around so fast, you can't focus on anything. The intensity of these symptoms indicates how catastrophic the consequences of failing appear to your unconscious.

As potentially devastating as fear can be to confidence, motivation and performance, you can learn to control yourself in the face of it. The first step is to recognize the warning signals that indicate that fear is affecting your performance. Just as there are signals on your automobile's dashboard to indicate trouble, we all have a set of inner signals to alert us that fear is taking charge. The quicker you become aware of these "warning signals," the faster you can initiate action that will transform fear's negative effects into positive action.

## MENTAL WARNING SIGNALS: SELF-TALK

We all talk to ourselves continually. "Don't forget to do this." "Why did I do that?" "If only I said that. . ." "What if this doesn't work?" " What if I bomb on this..."

When we're afraid or worried, these inner conversations, called self-talk, reflect fear and lack of confidence. This negative self-talk can be used as a warning signal.

The self-talk that warned me of a potential vicious cycle while writing this book was "You're not working fast enough. You'll never finish on time." The self-talk that caused Rachel to panic was "I should be available ; I'd better make the time." Peter's Drone Zone self talk was "I'm afraid my writing isn't going to be any good."

## RECOGNIZING SELF-TALK

You don't need to wait until you are scared or in a vicious cycle to uncover your negative self-talk. Listing some of your own warning signals now will make them easier to recognize when the pressure is on.

Situation (example): Running late for an appointment

Self-talk: "They're going to be really angry."

"They're not going to trust me. They'll think I'm a flake. They will never believe me."

"Dammit, why didn't I leave earlier?"

Before a presentation:

"How am I going to remember all these points?"

"I hope they don't ask about..."

"If I don't get this contract..."

Now, list your own examples and self-talk.

## BODY TALK: PHYSICAL WARNING SIGNALS

When Rachel feels overscheduled and then even more is asked of her, she says her insides feel like they're racing. "My forehead and palms sweat. I have trouble catching my breath. I'm doing everything at fast forward."

Peter, when sitting at his desk to write his screenplay, has an almost opposite response. "No matter what time it is, I feel sleepy. I find myself staring out the window, yawning and dreaming. And I just don't have any energy."

*"Body talk,"* your physical and behavioral responses when under pressure, is another type of warning signal indicating that a vicious cycle has begun.

## RECOGNIZING BODY TALK

Below are some typical body-talk warning signals. Check the ones you experience when under pressure. Add some of your own are not listed.

pain in the neck

headache

tightness in shoulders and chest

shortness of breath

clenched jaw

tight stomach

heart beating rapidly

 lower back pain

dizziness

dry mouth

tapping feet, pencils, fingers

catching your breath

sighing

shaky knees

procrastination

losing temper

feeling speedy

feeling "wired"

pacing the halls

## SUBSTITUTION RARELY WORKS

A common and understandable response when you catch your negative self-talk is to tell yourself to think positively. But trying to use positive self-talk to overcome fear or lack of confidence is usually fruitless. It's like putting on a clean shirt when you really need a shower—what's inside always seeps out.

Often the positive and negative self-talk will end up arguing with each other.

"Relax; you're going to be great in this interview. You've got all the qualifications."

"Yeah, but what if someone else is more qualified, or they like them better?"

"Don't sweat it. Take it easy. You're terrific. Just relax."

"How can I relax? If I don't get this job . . ."

Then if you do pay attention to one of these voices, it will be the one you believe, the one that has the most energy. And if you really believed the positive self-talk, you wouldn't have such a difficult job convincing yourself to think positively.

## STOP!

If your car's warning signal indicates trouble, ignoring it and continuing down the freeway is foolhardy and exacerbates the problem. Pulling off the road and stopping gives you the time to assess the situation and figure out a next step.

Similarly, the first thing to do once you have recognized your own warning signal is to *Stop!* Take a few slow, deep breaths. Hold each breath for a count of three, and exhale slowly. Just taking a few deep breaths will help you to calm down and regain some of your lost composure. "When my heart is pounding, I make myself breathe in slowly, hold it, and breathe out slowly," said Academy Award winning actor Jessica Tandy. "After a while, the heart stops pumping so fast, and I can go on." [10]

*"When you are in a hole, stop digging!"* was sage advice from Yogi Berra. When you are in the grip of fear, it is as if you are in a hole, so the key is to stop what you are doing. One exercise we teach people to use at these times is to take a few breaths, inhaling to the count of five and exhaling slowly to

the count of six. Doing that exercise three times has proven very effective for "stopping the digging."

Stopping for a moment and mentally stepping back also gives you more perspective about the situation. In effect, it distances you from the fear and prevents you from getting deeper into the Drone or Panic Zones. Just this simple little step can put *you*, rather than your fear, back in control of yourself and the situation.

Stopping provides the breather needed to re-evaluate the situation. It is now time to confront your fear to find out what is really going on—to do a reality check.

## CONFRONTING FEAR—LOOKING THE MONSTER IN THE EYE

"You gain strength, courage, and confidence by every experience in which you really stop to look fear in the face," said Eleanor Roosevelt.[11] A Southwestern American Indian tribe relates the following story to teach its children the importance of facing their fears.

Fear is like a 60-foot snake as big around as a ponderosa pine. Avoid it, and the snake grows larger and comes closer, rearing its huge ugly head, ready to strike. But if you look the snake in the eye, it sees its own reflection, gets scared, and shrinks away.

The remainder of this chapter discusses ways of looking the "monster in the eye" and transforming fear into confidence.

# CUTTING FEAR DOWN TO SIZE

Since almost all fears are exaggerated and irrational, they can be countered with a strong dose of reality. What is true about the situation, your ability to deal with it, and the consequences of not handling it? Your worst nightmare or your deepest concern is one thing, but the reality of what is most likely to happen is often quite another.

Reality checks put the kibosh on catastrophic thinking, horrific fantasies, and exaggerated consequences. The doomsday scenario-images of being fired and feelings of shame need to be examined and defused.

Many young swimmers entering the Olympic swimming arena for the first time freak out. The pool seems "too long and their distance too far," and they panic. Dara Torres has won four Olympic gold medals, and many silver and bronzes including a silver medal at the '08 Olympics at the age of 42. When she senses a rise in the stress levels of these "rookies," she helps to defuse the fear by reminding the young swimmers that the pool here is the *same size* as the ones they train in at home and that the distance of their races has not changed.[3]

A reality check won't change the difficulty of a situation. It won't turn a mountain into a molehill, but it will help you see what is really true about the situation. Fear makes a molehill seem like a mountain. A reality check will help you to see it for the molehill that it is or, in the case of the young Olympians, the same 50-meter length pool they have been working out in at home. This more accurate appraisal will often automatically diminish your fear.

A reality check is shifting from right brain thinking—which is great for creativity, but which also causes your fear-driven imagination to run wild—to more rational left-brain thinking.

The following four reality checks are methods for accurately assessing pressure situations.

## REALITY CHECK 1: IMAGINING THE WORST

Many people resist confronting their worst expectations. The possibilities seem so awful that they block them out and avoid thinking about them. This compounds the situation. The more you run from your fear the bigger it gets. Behind the curtain of fear, imagination invents all sorts of stories that, if unchallenged, will zap your confidence and general well-being.

"Before taking any risk, I always ask myself, 'What is the worst thing that can happen?' a vice president for a major telecom, told us. "Once I get a realistic idea of what that is, I decide whether I can live with these consequences or not. If I can, I go ahead and do it."

You can use this "worst-case scenario" reality check for any type of fear-driven situation. At one of our training sessions, Sara, L., a district sales manager for a telecom company, talked about the biggest challenge she faced. Like many managers, she admitted that it was difficult for her to handle problem people and to confront negative situations. She was currently anxious about telling one of her salespeople that he wasn't cutting it. "I keep putting it off, hoping he'll realize the what is happening and will somehow improve. But it's not. In fact, the more I put it off, the worse things are getting, and the harder it is for me to confront him.

A worst-case scenario check helped her realize that what *was* happening was far worse than the worst case that *could* happen if she confronted him.

At a follow-up session, she told me, "I did it! I talked to him, and you know what? He was actually relieved. Can you imagine that? He knew he wasn't performing well and had wanted to talk to me about it, but was feeling guilty and worried, so he kept putting it off. I tell you," she continued, "it was so much easier than I thought it would be. I've got three or four other things I've been avoiding; I can't wait to tackle them. I'm on a roll."

## REALITY CHECKING THE WORST CASE

The first step in using this technique is to check the likelihood of your expectations happening (on a scale of 1–10, will I really be fired if I am late?).

Remember the insurance exec in a previous chapter who jumped to the worst-case scenario, imagining the insurance industry as doomed, and he along with it, if a public insurance option became law? Well, I asked him, "On a scale of 1–10, how likely is that to happen?" After thinking a minute, he smiled sheepishly, saying, "Well, it is kind of ridiculous to think the insurance industry would be gone, but we'd definitely have to retrench and rethink some of our ways of doing business." And with that answer, his whole demeanor changed from being tense and stressed to more relaxed and thoughtful. "And that could be a challenge I'd love to sink my teeth in," he continued.

Another example of this very simple and valuable tool for dealing with fear happened when I was working with Alan B., a real estate developer, who felt stuck about his plans for expanding his business. "Every time I start planning to branch out, I stop" he told me.. The consequences of failing seem so scary that I don't want to think about them."

Here are some steps we took in this reality check:

1. "What's the worst thing that could happen if you failed?"

"I'm afraid I'll make some bad mistakes and go belly up. If that happened, I'd could easily lose everything I have—my equipment, my trucks, and maybe even my house, to say nothing of my reputation. Ugh! I don't even want to think about it!"

2. "On a scale of one to ten, how realistic is all that, with ten being certain that you'll go broke?" He stopped for a moment to reflect. "Well, I never thought of it that way before. It's probably only a four or, at the very most, a five." His whole body seemed to relax as he said those numbers. "That's not as bad as I thought, certainly not the debtors' prison I pictured myself going to a minute ago. Actually," he continued, looking more confident and resolved, "even if I did fail, I know I'd dust myself off and begin again. I'm highly skilled. Some of my competitors would probably be delighted if I closed my shop and would love to hire me."

The reality check helped Alan to see that the potential consequence of failing, although serious, wasn't nearly as catastrophic as he had scared himself into thinking. This realization broke the vicious cycle and allowed him to assess the situation realistically. Everything changed when he recognized that the consequences of failing weren't nearly as catastrophic as he'd imagined. The result—he had an expansion plan on his banker's desk within three weeks.

Dr. Charles Garfield, in his research on peak performers, found that most high-performing executives worked out a "catastrophic expectations report," either in their minds or in writing before taking a major risk. "They set out the worst that could possibly happen and decided whether they could possibly live with that outcome. If they could, they moved ahead confidently. Other executives," said Garfield, "didn't go through that process, and when taking a risk, tended to be hampered by a sense of impending doom."[12]

## REALITY CHECKING THE DIFFICULTY

Fear, as has been discussed, distorts your perception of the difficulty of a situation making everything seem harder than it is. To overcome this effect, the difficulty of many challenges you are confronting can be measured to see what is true about the situation.

There was always a point in an Inner Skiing Week when the skiers thought I had taken them to a slope that was too difficult. When I would ask them how steep they thought the slope was, their fear would exaggerate the steepness, and their answers would range from 50 to 70 degrees. If that were true, the slope would have been as steep as the face of El Capitan. I would then ask one of the skiers to do a reality check and measure the angle of the slope with his ski poles. He would invariably find that "It looks like about 20 to 25 degrees." The sigh of relief would be audible. As a result of this reality check, their fear would turn to enthusiasm, and they would start down the mountain without me. Seeing how steep the slope *actually was*, compared to what fear had caused them to *imagine*, decreased their stress level and increased their confidence.

That's the approach Dara Torres used with the young Olympians whose anxiety was causing them to imagine the pool as longer than it was.

## REALITY CHECKING THE OVERWHELM

Faced with a new and more daunting sales quota at the beginning of the year, many salespeople I have worked with, freak out. It seems Everestlike in scope and impossible to reach. I then have them do a reality check to see how many sales they *actually* have to make each month to reach the quota. Shifting from this seemingly impossible yearlong goal to more reasonable short-term goals eases their tension and increases confidence.

These days, with increasing amounts of information constantly bombarding us in the form of e-mails, faxes, twitters, reports..., people are feeling overwhelmed. The fear we won't keep up and get everything done can distort our perception and make our inner list seem twice as long and twice as hard as it really is. The result is that we end up in a frenzy in the Panic Zone or paralyzed in the Drone Zone. Either way, we have undercut our normal effectiveness, which makes our fears self-fulfilling.

To get a look at what you really have to do, move the list from *inside* your head to *outside*—on a piece of paper, your computer or a whiteboard. Making it visible and physically looking at what you actually have to do, as opposed to what your fear-fogged imagination is telling you, usually helps to calm you down and evaluate the situation more accurately. From a more composed mindset, you can then focus your attention on what you *are doing*, rather than on the self-talk about what *still* has to be done.

Using this type of reality check, "mountains" of paper, for instance, can be quickly sorted through to see how much really has to be done and when. Messages can be counted to see how many phone calls and e-mails really have to be made. Sales dollars can be totaled to see how much more you actually have to make to come in over quota.

## RATING THE DIFFICULTY

Another effective technique for doing a reality check is mentally rating the difficulty of the situation. This method has proven reliable in sports, in medicine, and in business for assessing and monitoring tension, pain, and stress levels.

When the mind is asked to rate something, for instance on a scale of 1–10, it breaks through distortions created by fear and becomes analytical and objective. I have seen any number of people literally petrified by their catastrophic expectations of what might happen if they take a risk. Yet, when asked to rate the difficulty of the task on a scale of 1–10, they become extremely rational. It's as if, at these times, they do a mental flip from the emotional right hemisphere of the brain to the more analytical and rational left hemisphere. The examples below and later in the chapter illustrate how to use ratings to assess a situation.

## RATING YOUR ABILITY—BRINGING THE PAST INTO THE PRESENT

Harold W. was in charge of writing promotion brochures for a fashion accessory manufacturer. Although he had a great deal of experience, he became anxious whenever he started a new brochure. He'd procrastinate almost to the deadline and then have to drive himself all the harder. "When I sit down to write, all I can think about is that maybe I won't come up with a fresh idea and I clutch."

I asked him to rate the difficulty of the brochure on which he was currently working, on a scale of 1–10. "It seems like an eleven," he joked. "Seriously, it's like I'm going to the gallows every time I sit down and think about the problem. All I want to do is run." "Have you ever done a job that seemed this difficult before?" I asked, encouraging him to use the past to evaluate the present situation. "Sure," he said. "Lots of them. They all seem this way." I asked him to recall a particularly difficult one. "It was the last one I did. We were introducing a quality line of accessories that was priced much higher than our competition. I had to position it at the top of the field, which was tough since the competition is very well established. But I came up with a unique approach and it got the best results of any piece I ever did." "Great," I said. "Now, remember the final piece, how it looked, and the results it got. What conclusion about your ability would you draw from that experience?" He looked around, a little embarrassed, and said, "I'm good when it comes to thinking up new ways of selling products." "OK, keeping that past success in mind, think about the new brochure you are working on. How would you rate the difficulty of this current piece?" "It's about an eight." He smiled and, already looking more confident, added, "But that's a challenge I can handle!"

When you are in the clutches of fear, you lose perspective. You think of past failures and future horrors. You forget that you have often been in similar situations and performed well. The difficulty of a situation and your ability to handle it can often be evaluated by looking through your memory bank for similar experiences and making a comparison.

Remembering past successes helps increase confidence and starts a vital cycle. Even when doing something new, there will always be familiar aspects. You might have never written a year-end report, but you probably have done many monthly reviews. You might never have spoken to

500 people, but you have given many speeches to smaller audiences. There is always some experience from which to gauge the difficulty. Having a positive reality base, grounding yourself in what you *do*, rather than don't, know and *have*, rather than haven't, done, helps to increase your confidence and control.

Even though the situation is no less difficult, the reality check calms you down. Once out of the grip of fear, you'll naturally be better at handling the challenge.

## BUT WHAT IF . . .

By doing a reality check, you will usually find that the situation isn't nearly as difficult as you thought, and the consequences are not catastrophic. But a reality check can also indicate that the situation *is* more than you can handle—the mountain is a mountain. In these cases, just having stopped to do the reality check will have given you a little distance from your fear so that you can consider options that you were too panicked to notice before. You can ask for more help, reset a quota, and reschedule a meeting or deadline. The only thing worse than a doomsday scenario is being unprepared for it.

## HOW TO STOP WORRYING

Most people are better at doomsday thinking than they are at contingency planning. Worry, not baseball, is really the national pastime. Worry and fear usually start with two words—*what if*—and then, the horror movie starts rolling.

You can stop that movie and shift anxiety into anticipation by changing the "what if" to "if... (it happens), then I can...."

For example,

> *What if* they don't like my proposal... to *if* they don't, *then* I will...
>
> *What if* I am fired... to *If* I am fired, *then* I will...
>
> *What if* I miss the plane... to *If I* miss it, then I will...

Changing worry to preparation is empowering. It frees up the energy stuck in imagining catastrophes and makes it available to create doable options,  which decreases your stress level and increases confidence.

## CREATIVE WORRYING

Sometimes, we encourage worrying. No, that's not a typo. We want people to worry. We want them to imagine all the things that might go wrong with a plan—and we mean everything! Down to the smallest and seemingly most mundane detail. "What if the name tags don't arrive on time, and if they do, suppose they are too big for the table we are setting them up on?"

After all the possible disasters are enumerated, we look at each and create a strategy for dealing with it. By the time we are done, every contingency has been explored. It's an incredibly energizing and upbeat exercise in problem solving that leaves people feeling empowered and confident. People learn two things from this exercise: how to control their worries and that just about every problem has a solution if you anticipate it, rather than wait for it to happen.

# THE REALITY CHECK EJECT BUTTON

The relief, energy, and renewed confidence you feel after doing a reality check imprints the exercise in your mind. With practice, you often won't even have to answer the question posed by your reality check. Simply asking it becomes like pushing an eject button that distances you from your fear and catapults you out of a vicious cycle.

At a follow-up session, Alan B., the developer, told us, "Whenever I notice I'm feeling panicked and in over my head, I stop for a second and take a deep breath. Then, I ask myself what's the worst thing that can happen? I no longer have to answer the question. Just asking it seems to short-circuit my panic. I immediately feel a sense of relief and can get on with what I want to do."

# BEING FEARLESSLY FOOLISH

*The key to overcoming fear and increasing confidence is not to think positively, but to think realistically.* A reality check is very different from positive thinking. Thinking positively can have negative results, depending on how you use it.

Convincing yourself that the sale you are about to pitch or the report you have to complete will be a cinch, when it won't be, can be detrimental to your performance and results. There's a big difference between being confident and being cocky. False confidence can cause you to underestimate the difficulty of a situation and overestimate your ability. The result is that you won't prepare as much, or as well, for the situation or have the energy and intensity that makes for a winning performance. You won't be as careful or diligent in what you say and do and you'll perform even worse than if you were scared.

Thinking positively, but not realistically, can cause you to overcommit or over challenge yourself. You end up like a cocky beginning skier who tries to ski an advanced slope. Because of his unrealistic confidence, he has gotten himself in over his head and out of control. A reality check, therefore, can help you not to be too relaxed and overconfident. A little anxiety is not a bad thing. It keeps you on your edge.

## FROM ANXIETY TO ACTION

You'll usually find, after doing a reality check, that a situation that seemed overwhelming will now seem challenging and possible. This shift in perception will change your attitude. You'll feel less anxious and tense, more confident and in control. The vicious cycle will have been broken, and you'll move naturally toward creating a vital cycle and ready for action.

## INCREASING CONFIDENCE— OVERCOMING FEAR

1. Select a high-pressure situation in which you'd like to feel more confident and be more effective.
2. What is your confidence level on a scale of 1–10?
3. List your **warning signals**. Consider both self-talk and body talk.

On recognizing these signals, remember to . . .

**Stop!**

**Breathe . . .**

Take three deep breaths. Hold each breath at the top for a count of three, and exhale slowly.

## REALITY CHECK

### *I. Rating the Difficulty of the Situation*

1. If possible, quantify the situation. How much really has to be done?

2. On a scale of 1–10, how difficult is this situation?

3. Have you ever had a similar experience? How difficult was it, on a scale of 1–10?

4. Based on this past experience, re-rate the difficulty of the present situation, on a scale of 1–10.

### *II: Rating the Consequences*

1. What is your catastrophic expectation?

2. Based on everything you know about yourself and the situation, how realistic is that, on a scale of 1–10, with 10 being definite?

3. If your answer is 6 or less, answer question number 5.

4. If your answer to no. 2 is more than 6, what plans can you make to prepare for such an eventuality?

5. What is your confidence level now, on a scale of 1–10?

# 9
# KEEP A VICTORY LOG

Faced with increased competition and tough shots, Tiger Woods always feels he can excel, "Over the course of my golf career, I've (been here) enough times where I can always say to myself, 'I've done this before; I've done it before. That gives you confidence."[1] What is he doing? Reflecting on a past success in a similar situation, which is another way to increase confidence and decrease debilitating stress.

Though most of us have both wins and losses, we tend to take our victories and *breakthroughs* for granted and remember the *breakdowns* much more vividly. You putt beautifully on seven greens, pretty good on a few others, and blow a three-footer. Which do you think about later? The one you blew. I've seen skiers who, after a minor fall at the beginning of a run, ski beautifully the rest of the way. Yet, at the bottom, they swear at themselves for having a bad run.

You respond to three questions in a meeting very well, one fairly well, and one you flub. Which are you thinking about as you leave the meeting? If you're human, it will be the one you blew. Then, this "negative" experience zaps your confidence and starts a vicious cycle.

Behavioral economists found that most people focus more on what they might lose rather than win, on the negative consequences of an act, rather than the positive opportunities. They also state that most feel the pain of losses more than the pleasure of gains.

## THE 10/90 SYNDROME

This tendency to focus on the negative exaggerates the mistake, blowing it out of proportion, and results in what I call the *10/90* response; the 10% of your performance that is poor becomes 90% in your mind. This inaccurate evaluation distorts your perception of reality, convincing you that you had an awful experience. Your confidence then plummets, affecting your mood as well as everything you do and everyone you relate to, often including your spouse and kids when you get home.

Then, when a similar situation next arises, the "awful" previous experience is most vivid in your memory bank. The response is to tense up and try too hard, or the opposite, to be overly cautious and tentative, either of which results in a poor performance. The vicious cycle continues, and it all started because of an inaccurate evaluation of a past event.

# PAST VICTORIES

If dwelling on fast failures saps your confidence and zaps your motivation, focusing on past successes achieves the opposite. Success is a great motivator and confidence builder. You confront a difficult challenge, succeed, feel great, and are motivated and excited about taking on the next one.

To help increase confidence and motivation as well as your performance and productivity, you can train yourself when going into a pressure situation, as Tiger Woods mentioned, to remember your past victories rather than your losses.

A vivid example of the effects of this type of thinking took place back in the 1988 Super Bowl in which the San Francisco 49ers were playing the Cincinnati Bengals. With less than two minutes left, the Niners were five points down with 90 yards to go for a touchdown. Looking at his players in the huddle, quarterback Joe Montana, one of sport's greatest pressure performers, is supposed to have said something to the effect of; "Hey, this is just like 1981."

What was he doing? Montana was reminding his teammates of a similar situation back in 1981 when the Niners were playing the Dallas Cowboys for the championship. Back then, with two minutes remaining, Montana led the team the length of the field, and in the final seconds, threw a game- and championship-winning touchdown pass.

Reflecting on that experience, Montana got his teammates to realize that not only had they *been in a similar situation before*, but also that they had been successful in it. Remembering that past victory over Dallas calmed the players down and increased their confidence. The result was that they went down the field, and in the waning seconds of the game, Montana threw the touchdown pass that beat the Cincinnati Bengals and S.F. won the Super Bowl.

## "GREAT REMINDER"

When University of California wide-receivers coach Kevin Daft spliced together a video of Cal receivers' top plays from training camp, he thought seeing the highlights would build their confidence. It did much more than that.

Hours after watching the 68-play video of their great plays, the receivers created a highlight reel performance in the next game. They combined for 10 catches, 215 yards, and 2 touchdowns in a 52–13 trouncing of Maryland.

"After we saw that tape, it was obvious that we had so much potential that we had been wasting," said Cal's leading receiver, Nyan Boareng. "We knew the sky was the limit for us, but we had to go out and do it and build on it and get better." [2]

## LOOKING BACK

When I taught skiing, I would watch skiers, halfway down a difficult run, stop and look down the rest of the slope with dread. I'd then encourage them to look *back up* the hill at the tough turns they had *already* made. The change in attitude was instantaneous. Looking at what they had already accomplished increased their confidence about skiing the rest of the run.

There is nothing like winning to create a winning attitude. The more you remind yourself of past victories and successes, the more you'll build a positive reality base for handling challenging situations. This is one reason we always encourage people to celebrate victories.

## NOT POSITIVE THINKING

Focusing on past victories, as has been discussed, isn't positive thinking, nor is it dreaming, just hoping that you will do well. Reflecting on past victories is *reality thinking.* It's not maybe you can; it's that you *already* have. The successes you have had are *real.* They *did happen*—and remembering them increases your confidence and creates positive momentum.

Reality thinking involves accurately evaluating your efforts. Count the good shots as well as the bad, the great responses as well as the flubs. Balancing the losses with the wins provides you with a realistic view of your efforts. If you're like most people, you aren't giving yourself credit for being as good as you are.

I'm not saying you should ignore the mistakes, errors, and failures. They present great opportunities for learning and growing. But when we dwell and obsess on them, they are blown out of proportion.

## VICTORY LOGS AND HIGHLIGHT FILMS

To increase confidence and motivation for any situation, ranging from sports to work to school, I recommend keeping a victory log and, if applicable, even a personal highlight film to record your past wins.

Keeping a victory log will enable you to build a positive reality base for successfully handling tough situations. Reading your victory log before pressure situations will increase your confidence, turn your anxiety into excitement, and enable you to perform at peak levels more often.

Entries into your victory log don't have to be long or detailed. A line or even a word or two can evoke a memory and the accompanying feeling. The act of making note of these positive experiences, putting them down on paper, I have found, makes them more real and imprints them more deeply in the psyche.

I keep a victory log of the times when I was in the Peak Zone giving a speech. Flipping through it before each presentation gets me more energized and confident. I get the feeling that Tiger said, "Hey, I've been here before and done well."

"I used to be panicked before my monthly presentations to the board," the president of a major software company told me. After a coaching consult, he decided to keep a victory log. Following each meeting, he would jot down reminders about the wins he had in that meeting. "Now, prior to every presentation, I thumb through my victory log, which helps to calm me down and feel more confident and ready."

Nordstrom's, one of the most successful department store chains, noted for their spectacular customer service, has a motto of "Respond to Unreasonable Customer Requests." This credo, which has resulted in salespeople doing the out of the ordinary such as hand delivering items to the airport for a customer's last-minute business trip, changing a customer's flat tire, or paying his or her parking ticket. Nordstrom's encourages these acts by keeping scrapbooks of "heroic" acts.

## ON THE WALL

Susan Harris, a telemarketer for a well-known San Diego playhouse, came up with a unique form of victory log. "Every time I make a sale, I draw a heart in color on the card, write the date and amount of the sale on the heart, and tack it onto my wall. Then, whenever I feel myself going into a slump or losing energy, I take a break and look at my victory wall. Focusing on my successes," she told me, "reminds me that I know what I am doing, doing it well, and that the product is exceptional. The result is that my brief victory wall break re-energizes and inspires me, and my confidence and enthusiasm return."

"Looking at all those victories has never failed to bring me out of a slump," says Harris who, since starting her victory wall has become the number one salesperson for the playhouse. Her problem now is that "I am running out of space on the wall. I guess they'll have to give me a bigger office."

## IMPROVING YOUR LIFE

Victory logs can help improve the quality of your life as well as your performance. When John Ernst was the CEO of a major advertising agency, he did a daily review before going to bed. Most of the review, he said, consisted of what didn't go right and what he'd have to fix the next day. "As a result, I'd feel frustrated, anxious, depressed, and wasn't sleeping," he told me.

"Keeping a victory log, first of all, helped me to realize that we were doing much better than I thought. But more than that, this simple little exercise changed everything—my work and my life. I'm much more positive, upbeat, and easier to be around now. And I like myself better."

## STARTING YOUR VICTORY LOG

Tear out the following page and use its message to start your victory log.

The internal rewards of victory are joy, vitality, well-being, and the knowledge that, throughout your life, you will continue to exceed your own limits and break your own records.

Before you close this book, remind yourself of a past success. See it in your mind's eye. Feel it. Experience your power. Remind yourself that the potential to perform at this level, to live at this level, is always there waiting to be experienced and expressed in everything you do, wherever you go.

Throughout your life, you will have numerous successes. You will accomplish goals, have moments of great clarity and vision, and some of your dreams will come true.

———————————

This VICTORY LOG is a special place for you to record these personal victories.

———————————

Read your VICTORY LOG from time to time. It will remind you of your accomplishments and help you remember how terrific you really are.

———————————

Your VICTORY LOG will give you insights into your strengths and get you back on track when you are in a slump or running on empty.

———————————

Read your VICTORY LOG before a big presentation, embarking on a major project, or before any pressure situation. You will find it a source of confidence, inspiration, and power.

———————————

Reminding yourself of your past victories helps you identify with your potential rather than your problems. It enables you to act from a position of strength rather than weakness, to feel more powerful, confident, and in control of yourself in any situation.

———————————

Each limit exceeded, each boundary crossed, verifies that most limits are self-imposed, that your potential and possibilities are far greater than you have ever imagined, that you are capable of far more than you have ever thought.

# 10
# DOING WHAT COMES NATURALLY

"I'm really nervous about this upcoming speech. I'm basically a shy person and speaking to 300 people is really panicking me, and the 30 minutes I have seems like 50 hours," Lenore Lefer told me. Ms. Lefer is a nationally known psychotherapist who has worked for the past 20 years with people dealing with cancer, told me. She had been invited to be the keynote speaker at an international conference on cancer and sexuality. "I'm used to doing interactive programs of 10 or 12 and can do that with my eyes closed. I'm also really good when I'm doing Q&A for a larger audience, but just giving a speech to them scares me."

I then suggested framing her speech to do what she did best and felt most comfortable with, which was Q&A. "Why not start with the Q&A," I suggested, "by saying something like; 'the 5 questions I am most often asked are...' and then answering them, just as if you were doing a real Q&A."

She was delighted with that possibility, and in an e-mail I received after her presentation, she wrote, "The speech went great! I got terrific feedback."

Nothing zaps your confidence and motivation as much as trying to do things for which you aren't naturally suited. Bruce Hubby, the chairman of Professional Dynametric Programs, whose surveys for evaluating people have been used by more than 5,000 companies and 3 million people, says, "When people feel the need to act unnaturally, they experience the stress which lowers productivity and leads to job dissatisfaction. People are at their most productive when they're in a position that lets them draw on their natural strengths."[1]

## DON'T SHORE UP WEAK SPOTS

We've all received the well-meaning advice that if we want to excel, we need to shore up our weak spots and round out our game, or that if we want to move up in the organization, we have to learn new skills. Sounds good, but this strategy doesn't work when the skills you are trying to improve aren't ones for which you are naturally suited. Trying to get an introvert to be a good salesperson is never going to be successful. The most achieved when trying to improve in an area that is not a basic strength is mediocrity, and that ain't going to get you to first base.

Babe Ruth probably could have learned to bunt, but that wasn't his strength or the job he was paid to do.

# THE GLORIES OF THE MESSY DESK

Shortly after starting my motivational speaking business, my wife Marilyn came into my office and was shocked when she looked at my desk, which looked as if a hurricane had just hit. "You've got to get organized or the only thing you're going to succeed at is making a bigger mess," she told me.

I agreed, got an organizational consultant to work with me, and learned a lot of good stuff about getting myself organized, for example, "Clean your desk at the end of the day; have an ABC list on your computer ready to start the day when you come in; handle each paper once; don't just lay it on your desk with all the rest of the things you are 'going to get to later.'" And I took the lessons to heart.

When she returned in a month to review my progress, she asked me how things were going. I said I noticed three things:

1. I was definitely more organized.
2. I had an incredible headache.
3. I hadn't written one new speech or article or made a new sales call all month. All I seemed to be doing was getting myself organized.

Then, the light bulb went on. 'Kriegel, organization isn't your game. Your game is selling, writing, speaking.' Now, when I come into my office, and it's a mess, I feel good, knowing that I must have been doing something important the day before.

"If you try to become proficient at what you are weak at, it takes an inordinate amount of time. That means you don't have time to keep improving at what you are already good at, so that skill gets rusty, and you end up mediocre at everything," said executive coach Sandy Mobley, a former manager of training at companies like McKinsey and Hewlett-Packard, who founded the Learning Advantage, told me. " the so-called well rounded personality," she explained, ' is really in my experience very, very rare."

"Don't focus on building your weaknesses. Understand your strengths, and place yourself in a position where these strengths count," advised management guru Peter Drucker. "Your strengths are what will carry you through to success."[2]

Working on your strengths is also more enjoyable, making it more motivating to improve and excel. The rapid success you achieve by maximizing your strengths further improves your confidence and motivation, which then leads to more success. A positive vital cycle is created.

## DIFFERENT LADDERS

"This all sounds good, but if I want to make more money and be more successful, I have to move up to management and probably improve in areas I'm not skilled at" is a typical response I hear. OK, let's say you do move up to management, and it isn't your thing. Thomas K. is a typical example. A top engineer for a telecom company, he had recently been promoted to V.P. of the division. The new position required managing a staff of more than 150 people which involved keeping them motivated and performing well. It also involved giving major presentations to top management and clients.

Then, there were the usual management responsibilities of forecasting, budgeting, staffing and recruiting, keeping costs in line, and mountains of paper.

Although Tom was great at solving intricate problems and developing innovative new designs, he was basically an introvert, uncomfortable with people and terrified of giving large presentations. He also had little patience for all the paperwork his new job required. Wanting to succeed in his new position, he set out to improve these skills. He took presentation workshops, hired a speaking coach, and even enrolled in a basic accounting course at a local university. Although he improved, he never really became comfortable with all the presentations and people duties and continued to view the paperwork as his nemesis.

The bottom line was that Tom went from a job he loved and at which he excelled to one he disliked, and which at best would never be better than mediocre. After a year of trying to adapt, he went on a leave of absence and, eventually, took a job as the chief design engineer with a competitor.

Promoting from strength to weakness occurs more often than you can imagine. A top salesperson is promoted to sales manager, a position requiring very different skills and temperament and not only doesn't like it, but also performs poorly. Similarly, many entrepreneurs fail miserably when they try to manage what they have started. Managing a business requires a completely different set of skills and attitude than starting it did. The same phenomenon is true in sports, where rarely does the great athlete excel at managing.

# DIFFERENT LADDERS

When you're in a position you're not suited for, you have to work twice as hard just to reach a level of competency and keep your head above water. And if you're just competent at what you are doing, you ain't going to be there for long. Luckily, today, some companies, recognizing this phenomenon and wanting to keep people in positions in which they can excel, have created a new type of corporate ladder.

Eric B. was a top salesperson for a major life insurance company. Rather than promote him to management, which they knew he wasn't cut out for, they created a senior position in which he could still do what he loved and did best, which was call on clients. "I love the challenge of face to face selling" he told me.

But the new job, for which he received a substantial bump in salary, benefits, and perks, also consisted of coaching new salespeople by taking them on sales calls, giving speeches at sales meetings, helping to motivate the sales force, and working with those in a slump. Eric enjoyed, excelled at, and was already doing these jobs in an unofficial capacity, anyway.

With this move, the company benefited by having Eric out in the field and still producing. But they also got the opportunity to have him use his expertise and charisma, to help in the training, development, and motivation of the sales force. As a result, he not only increased his income, but also got to continue doing what he loved and did best. Double win.

# FOR LEADERS AND COACHES—DON'T IMPROVE WEAKNESSES

The same philosophy works when coaching. Based on interviews with more than 80,000 managers, Marcus Buckingham and Curt Coffman of the Gallup Organization, the authors of the best-selling book, *First Break All the Rules,* found that great managers "focus on each person's strengths and manage around his weaknesses. Don't try to fix the weakness. Don't try to perfect each person. Instead, do everything you can to help each person cultivate his talents. Help each person become more of who he already is."[3]

"You don't need to know about people's weaknesses;" adds Bruce Hubby, "you need to know about their strengths. Trying to correct a person's weaknesses can be a demotivator. People gain confidence when you build on their strengths."[4]

Bill Walsh, often called a genius, won four Super Bowls as coach of the San Francisco 49ers, and he is recognized as one of the greatest coaches ever. At a meeting analyzing prospective draft picks, Walsh told his scouts, when reporting on prospects, not to tell him about a player's weaknesses, but his strengths.

Best Buy CEO Brad Anderson advises creating the right job for talented employees. "We're put on Earth with a given set of skills," said Anderson. Someone might not be good at sales, but be strong at building a team. As a leader, you need to learn to adjust to those strengths and assign people a job fitting their talent.[5]

We are all different. We each have different talents, skills, aspirations, goals, and dreams. The role of a leader or a coach is to know the strengths of every team member and see that each person works at something that enables him to turn his passions and natural talents into expertise and peak performance.

## THE ODD COUPLE

Many people try to improve  by copying another person's strengths. We find a role model and emulate this person who has the skills, the ìstyle,î or the attitude that we think we need to develop.  The futility of this is something I learned awhile ago.

When *Inner Skiing* was published, my coauthor, Tim Gallwey, the author of the best selling Inner books, The Game of Tennis and Inner Golf, and I scheduled promotional events around the country.  Expecting 50, we found that over 500 people showed up at our first program.  I had never given a speech before a large audience and was petrified. So Tim went first.  He proceeded to sit on one of the  chairs on the stage and just talked calmly and eloquently for about 30 minutes. He was awesome!

Using Tim as my model, I too, pulled up a chair and tried to emulate his relaxed, thoughtful style.  I used the same approach, sat in the same damn chair, in front of the same audience, yet while he was great, I bombed.

If you knew Tim and me you would immediately understand how ludicrous it would be for either of us to try to emulate the other.  Tim basically is reserved and intellectual, whereas

I am more enthusiastic and speak with lots of expression and body language. We are, truly, the odd couple. On hindsight, trying to copy Tim was ridiculous because in îfinding him,î I lost myself.

## DON'T BE A 'WANNABEE'

'Wannabeeî' is an expression for those who 'want to be' like someone else. They mimic the way their hero dresses, talks, and walks, affect the same mannerisms, everything. There are Madonna wannabees, Elvis wannabees, Michael Jackson wannabees.

You've seen it at work, too. There are the îbossî wannabees who mirror those in a position of power. They wear the same kinds of clothes as the boss, effect the boss's mannerisms, walk like the boss, talk like the boss, and if the boss smokes a pipe, off they go to the smoke shop.

In my speech I was a Tim wannabee. The problem with being a wannabee is no matter how much you may *wanna*bee like that other person, you ain't *gonna* be! A good carbon copy is still a copy, and is nowhere near as good as an original. I was a lukewarm version of Tim. Trying to use what worked for him, I didn't use what worked for me. As a result I didn't make the most of my own strengths, my own uniqueness. If you become a wannabee you will never be more than second best. No one is better than the original. And in a laser-fast world, second best isn't good enough.

# FOCUSING ON CORE COMPETENCIES

Businesses of all kinds today are being redefined and reinvented with this strategy in mind. They are lopping off those areas that are not their strengths and focusing on core competencies. Telcom giants AT&T, Verizon, and Sprint don't manufacture their phones or cables. Instead, they focus on their strengths, such as innovative approaches to marketing, product design and customer service. The same is true for people, focusing on your own core competency will increase your confidence and help you to be more motivated and performing at peak levels.

# STRENGTH ASSESSMENT

Take a minute and write down three of your strengths or "core competencies." Your strengths, or core competencies, are natural personality traits such as creativity, empathy, outgoingness, analytical skills, listening skills, and the ability to inspire people. Your strengths are qualities that can be expressed in almost any type of situation, work or play.

1.  To obtain a clear picture of your strengths, circle three of the words below that most describe you and combine them.

    Extrovert, Introvert, Creative, Analytical, Intuitive, Energetic, Staid, Positive, Cynical, Actor, Thinker, Starter, Finisher, Restless, Comfortable, Excitable, Calm, Risk Taker, Cautious, Great with People, Great Problem Solver, Loquacious, Quiet

2. Review some of your accomplishments. What were the main qualities enabling you to achieve them?

3. Since loving to do something is usually a sign of a core competency, what are some of your hobbies, things you gravitate to in your spare time. What personal qualities do these activities give you an opportunity to express? For instance, mountain climbing might indicate a love of adventure and risk taking; doing crossword and jigsaw puzzles, a love of problem solving and working out details.

4. Write a quarter-page classified ad for yourself.

## LEADING FROM STRENGTH

Using your strengths increases your confidence, which will enable you to be more productive and to perform better, as well as making work more enjoyable. And when you have more fun, you are more creative, more motivated, and more effective.

The following exercises will help you improve your confidence, effectiveness, and enjoyment of your work.

Think of your current work:

- Are you using your strengths in this job—where and when?

- Where are some opportunities for you to use your strong points further?

- How could you redesign your job so that you make more use of your core competencies?

- Design the perfect work for you, making the most of your strengths. Write the job description.

## GO FOR GREAT!

Remember, working on improving your weaknesses takes longer, is harder, and is less productive. Although this strategy might get you to become competent, being good at what you do isn't good enough. To excel, it's important to identify and build on your strengths. Peak performers aren't good at many things; they are great at one or two. Remember, the Babe never bunted.

# 11
# CONQUERING SABOTAGE THINKING

Without realizing it, many of us unwittingly sabotage our own best efforts. We mentally rehearse our own failure by spending far too much time focused on the things we don't want to have happen.

We were working with Carl J., a young lawyer, before his first trial. Although he had prepared diligently, he found himself becoming increasingly nervous and stressed as the trial date approached. After he outlined the situation, I asked him what specifically he was worried about.

"I don't want to appear young and inexperienced. And I certainly don't want them to think this is my first trial."

Carl's problem was not his inexperience, but that he had fallen victim to the **don'ts**, which is a form of sabotage thinking. Whein thinking about what you don't want to do or don't want to have happen, you are unconsciously doing a negative mental rehearsal. Ironically, thinking about what you don't want to have happen will often make it happen.

Harvard psychologist Daniel Wegner wrote that the unconscious attempt to avoid errors consistently increases their likelihood of occurring. The same happens with words and thoughts, as it does with actions. Tell someone "don't think of a white bear," and, almost certainly, for the next 10 minutes, white bears are all he or she is thinking about.

If you tell a person not to think of a given word and then give them a word association test under time pressure, they are likely to blurt out the forbidden word as a response. The concentrated attempt not to think about it becomes just another way of thinking about it. Wegner calls it the "ironic return of repressed thoughts."

In one experiment, researchers put eye-tracking cameras on soccer players and instructed them to avoid a part of the goal in making a penalty kick. Guess where their gazes most often fell?[1]

Often a group in my Inner Skiing programs would tell me they wanted to ski the trees-- to to go off the groomed slope to ski the area with lots of trees. I would then tell them they didn't want to ski the trees, but the spaces between them.

## J. P.'S NOSE

Many years ago, George Wheelwright, a founder of Polaroid, told me that when he was trying to get investment capital for the company, J.P. Morgan was interested and had invited George and his family to dinner. Wheelwright was nervous because Morgan had a reputation as being very ornery. He was also very sensitive about his nose, which was purported to be like W. C. Field's—big, bulbous, and red-veined. So, before the dinner, Wheelwright instructed his young daughter, "Don't stare at his nose; don't say anything about it; and don't even mention the word *nose*."

The evening went smoothly, and Morgan was warm and friendly. But when the butler served the dessert and coffee, Wheelwright's little daughter picked up the sterling silver sugar and creamer, went up to Morgan, and in the cutest little voice asked, "Mr. Morgan, how many lumps of sugar would you like... in your nose?"

## EVEN THE PROS DO IT

Detroit Tigers pitcher Justin Verlander was the 2006 rookie of the year, has been a two time all-star, and has thrown a no-hitter. Yet even pros such as Verlander fall into the *don'ts* trap at pressure times. In the World Series against the Cardinals, Verlander picked up a bunt by Jeff Weaver with runners on first and second and had only one idea. "I thought to myself, 'Don't throw it away.' So, guess what happened. 'I threw it in the tank,"[2] he said. His wild throw down the left field line led to a two-run inning.

## MENTAL MOVIES

Little Miss Wheelwright was so well versed and coached in the *don'ts* that she didn't know what to *do*, just as the golfer preparing for a shot thinks, "Don't hit it into the water!" Where is his shot most likely to go? Right, kerplunk! Same is true in anything. You go into a meeting thinking, 'Don't look at the boss's bobbing Adams apple' or into a presentation telling yourself; 'not to look at that guy who's not paying attention.' Guess where you look?

The reason for this response is that what's foremost in your mind at these times is what *not to do*. And since your mind controls your behavior, you tend to act out what you are thinking about -- hitting the ball into the lake; staring at the boss's Adams Apple or the guy who's yawning. Bottom line— thinking about what you don't want to happen increases the chances it will happen.

## BEATING THE DON'TS

I learned about how to beat the don'ts from a Native American teammate of mine on the New York Lacrosse Club. Several members of his tribe had come to the city to work construction on the tall buildings because they had no fear of heights. I did have a fear of heights, at the time, so I asked him for advice.

Rather than tell me what to do, he took me up to the roof in his apartment house which was about 8 stories high. He then walked me close to the edge and instructed me to *look down*. I immediately became dizzy, and was terrified. My stomach was jumping, and my legs were like shaving cream. Then, he told me to look across to the roof of another building a block away. I was now looking out, rather than down. No problem. No butterflies. Then, he said, with a big smile, something so simple and appropriate that I have used in every area of my life and, especially, in my speeches. He told me, *"Don't look where you don't want to go."*

I have often used this technique with skiers reluctant to take a steep chair lift because of their fear of heights. After coaxing them to take the lift, I would ask them when we got to the highest point and they were beginning to panic, "Where are you looking?" "Down!" they would shriek. "Now, look out to the horizon," I would tell them. Simple as that, the butterflies flew away.

## POSITIVE TARGETING

Before going into a pressure presentation or, for that matter, any situation, rather than focusing on a negative target—the don'ts—give yourself a positive target. Think about what you *do* want to do rather than what you *don't*, how you *do* want to appear, and what you *do* want to have happen.

Reed Hastings, the founder and CEO of Netflix, founded his first company, Puree Software, in 1991 when he was 31. As the company grew from 10 to 40 to 120 to 320 to 640 employees, "I found I was definitely underwater and over my head. I was doing white water kayaking at the time, and in kayaking, if you stare and focus on the problem, you are much more likely to hit danger. But I learned to focus on the safe water and what I wanted to happen."[3] Transferring this learning to his work, Puree Software became very successful and was acquired in 1997, after which, he founded Netflix.

## DON'TS TO DO'S

"How do you want to appear in the courtroom?" I asked Carl J., the young lawyer discussed in the first part of this chapter.

"I want to look professional, self-assured, like I know what I am talking about," he replied.

I asked him to tell me what "self-assured" would look like. To him, it meant he would move confidently, use convincing body language, make eye contact with the witnesses, especially the jury, and project his voice so that it could be heard from the bench to the back of the courtroom.

"Show me what this would look like," I asked.

He then acted out these characteristics so rather than just words and mental concepts, they became things he could *do.* In effect, he was rehearsing how he wanted to be, rather than focusing on how he didn't. His confidence soared, " Hey I can definitely do that" he said with a smile.

We used to use this exercise when teaching skiing. When we would ask skiers their goals for the run they were about to take, a typical response was, "I don't want to feel so tight," or "I don't want to look like a klutz."

We'd then ask them how they'd like to ski, rather than how they wouldn't. Not feeling so tight would then turn into "I want to feel more relaxed." And not looking like a klutz turned into "I want to be smooth." We'd then ask them to *show* us what skiing more relaxed or smooth would look like. You're not going to believe this, but it's true—lo and behold, they would do it, ski the way they wanted to. "Oh, that's the way you'd like to ski, eh?" we'd ask. And the look of surprise, when they got what had just happened, was golden.

## MENTAL CHECK

The first step to overcoming sabotage thinking is to recognize when you are doing it. So, before your next presentation or any pressure situation, do a mental check. *Think about what you are thinking about.* Do you have a clear positive target, on what you want to do, or are you worried and focused on what you don't?

The next chapter will teach you how to do the positive mental rehearsal that will enable you to excel in any upcoming situation.

# 12
# MENTAL TRAINING: PROGRAMMING YOURSELF FOR THE PEAK ZONE

When I asked the world-class athletes I worked with, "How important is your mental game to your performance?" the response I would always get was well over 60%. Yet, when I asked how much mental training they did, I would always get a blank stare.

In a conversation with Dr. Gregory Raipport, a former psychiatrist for the Russian Olympic team, I got a very different response. Speaking about mental training, he told me, "With us, it is a science," and he outlined a test they had done several years back. Before a previous winter Olympic Games, the Russians divided athletes into four groups with different ratios of mental to physical training.

| | % PHYSICAL TRAINING | % MENTAL TRAINING |
| --- | --- | --- |
| Group A | 100 | 0 |
| Group B | 75 | 25 |
| Group C | 50 | 50 |
| Group D | 25 | 75 |

The improvement in performance for each group was then measured over time. The group that showed the best incremental improvement was Group D, those athletes who spent 75 percent of their time practicing mentally and 25 percent physically.

When under pressure, most of us are usually only aware of thoughts, such as "I've gotta be great or else...," "If I don't finish this...," or "Uh oh, they look..." or physical sensations, such as sweaty palms or a pounding heart. But it is our unconscious *mental images* of how we will perform that create our thoughts, feelings, and the resulting behavior. "Feedforward" is the term Stanford neurophysiologist Karl Pribram uses to describe the images of achievement and misachievement that precede and affect all our actions.

In other words, your mind works in pictures. These mostly unconscious mental images create the thoughts, shape your attitude, and guide your behavior. The late Italian psychiatrist Roberto Assagioli wrote in *The Act of Will* that "images and mental pictures tend to produce the physical conditions and the external acts that correspond to them."

An image in the mind fires the same neural connections in the autonomic nervous system as an actual experience. As a result, research has shown that the body can't distinguish between an actual experience and a clearly held and deeply imprinted image. In a test done with Olympic track athletes, a clearly held mental image fired the same neural connections as an actual experience would. *Your mind perceives visualizing yourself performing in your Peak Zone as real.* Therefore, mental rehearsal, or visualization as it is commonly called, serves as an effective tool for imprinting peak performance patterns.

## MAXIMIZING PERFORMANCE

There have been many experiments indicating the positive effects of visualization. George Sheehan, in his book, *On Running*, wrote of a test study done by Canadian physicians, in which they divided post-coronary patients into two groups. One group was given a program of daily jogging and exercise. The other only did mental imagery. "They imagined themselves jogging or pictured themselves in a beautiful meadow filling their lungs with wonderful fresh air and feeling the oxygen going through the whole body reaching the heart."[1]

After a year, the results were identical for both groups. Weight and body fat were down. There was an increase in grip strength and EKG tracings. Blood pressure was lowered, and adrenaline production by the body was lowered.

Equally dramatic are the results of a research study involving three groups of students, chosen at random, shooting basketball foul shots. One group physically practiced foul shots for 30 minutes a day. The second group did nothing. The third group visualized themselves shooting foul shots for 20 minutes a day. At the end of 20 days, the first group, which had practiced every day, improved 24 percent. The second group, which had done nothing, showed no improvement. The third group, which had only visualized themselves shooting fouls, improved 23 percent![2]

Golfing great Jack Nicklaus attributed 10 percent of his success to his setup, 40 percent to his stance and swing, and 50 percent to the mental imagery he used before taking a swing.[3]

Nicklaus is only one of the many world-class athletes who use visualization, the technique for creating and controlling mental images to prepare for pressure situations. Baseball Hall-of-Famer Joe Morgan visualized himself swinging a bat "even when I'm in the bathtub."[4] Phil and Steve Mahre, winter Olympic gold and silver medalists in the slalom, were seen on international television visualizing their runs as they waited in the starting line. The list of world-class athletes who use visualization to maximize performance would sound like a Who's Who of sporting greats..

## IMPROVING MENTAL PERFORMANCE

Visualization works for more than just sports. It is very effective for increasing confidence and preparing for any type of situation, mental or physical. Top performers in business, politics, medicine, law, and the arts, whom we interviewed, all used mental imagery to prepare for pressure situations.

Former Time Inc CEO Dick Munroe told us that, as part of his preparation, for an important speech, he would imagine the whole environment. "I will see in my mind what it would look like, who would be there, how they'd be seated, and how I wanted to come across."[4]

"Windmilling" is what Bettina Parker calls her process of mental rehearsal. When Ms. Parker, the former president of a large international marketing and consulting firm, was working on an important project, she visualized it all in her head and rehearsed it until it played out perfectly. She'd often practice like this for days before a meeting to make sure she had everything worked out just right.[5]

The rest of the chapter will teach you different ways to use visualization to program yourself for Peak Zone performance. Imaging yourself performing in that zone will help to imprint that behavior and make it your automatic response to any pressure situation.

## RE-VIEWING 1: YOUR PERSONAL HIGHLIGHT FILM

Tom McMurphy, a former small-college All-American basketball player who is now a successful insurance salesman told us that whenever he had a big game coming up, he would review in his mind his "personal highlight film." "I would visualize the tough games I had played really well in. Watching these old tapes gave me confidence and got me psyched up.

"I do the same thing now in selling," McMurphy said.

"When I have to make an important presentation and am feeling nervous about it, I mentally rerun one of my selling 'highligh' films. I visualize the last time I made a successful presentation. If I have time, I might even run several of them. Running these old tapes in my mind gives me confidence by reminding of some of the really good experiences I've had."

A recent research study indicated the effectiveness of a personal highlight film for improving performance. A videotape focusing on a professional basketball player's great moves—his slam dunks, great passes, perfect assists—was prepared. The player watched the tape 20 times over a 30-game period. His point production for that period increased 41 percent! His steals per game increased 60 percent![6]

Visualizing your own inner highlight film and watching it before you go into pressure situations will help to increase your confidence and program you for a peak performance. Most of us already have enough material to make up our own highlight film. More than 90 percent of the people who attend our management seminars report previous successes in the same types of situation that presently cause them stress.

Visualizing a Peak Zone experience creates a chain reaction. When you image a past success, you imprint that experience in your mind, increasing your confidence that you **can do** it again, and initiating a vital cycle.

# RE-VIEWING 2: SHIFTING FEELINGS

"I'm not tough enough when I need to be," Ian, a literary agent, told me. "I work out great deals for my clients on paper, but I'm terrible at face-to-face negotiations. I never want to ruffle any feathers or make anyone angry. When things get tough, I have a tendency to get nice. And because I'm too easy, I'm not as effective as I could be."

"How would you like to be?" I asked him.

"Tough," he said, and then added, "and independent, not concerned with what people think of me."

Ian couldn't remember ever having been tough and independent in a negotiation session. So, I asked him if he had performed with these qualities at any other time in his life.

He thought for a minute and then said, "The picture that came to my mind was when I was on the tennis team in college. I was great at the net. My volleys were real hard and, sometimes, aimed right at my opponent. I wasn't worried about being liked. I wanted to win. I was the captain of our team in my senior year, and played no #1.. I was smart and tough as a player. That's exactly the way I'd like to be for my clients."

I had Ian mentally re-view scenes from his tennis experience and focus on his attitude. Images create feelings. Re-viewing an old mental tape will help you to re-experience *the feeling* you had at that time. As Ian reran his old tennis tapes, his jaw became firmer and set, his mouth tightened, and his face looked more serious. He even sat straighter. In a 15-minute visualization exercise, he had transformed into a formidable, determined, and intimidating-looking individual.

I then had him visualize a past negotiation but this time, with the feeling and attitude he had on the tennis court. Afterwards, he said, "That's exactly how I want to be in those situations—strong, tough, give no quarter. I can be liked later," he joked.

Feelings and attitudes are transferable. If you have expressed them in one area of your life, they can be expressed in other areas as well. Ian now had a highlight film that he could use to prepare himself for future negotiating sessions.

Laurie K., a successful manager of rock music groups, used the same technique to motivate herself for tasks that she didn't like to do. She loved playing squash and would often play a couple of games before going to the office. This would give her a lot of energy and enthusiasm, which she'd then automatically bring to the job. When she didn't have time to play, she'd take five minutes or so imagining herself playing. "I'll always remember a tight game, one in which I played real well. I'll run through the great points I made. After doing this mental exercise, I'll feel strong and full of energy. Making those phone calls I had dreaded would then seem easy."

## MAKING YOUR HIGHLIGHT FILM

The first step to creating your personal highlight film is to recall a relevant experience when you were at your best. Select either the same type of situation or one in which you have experienced, as Ian did, the attitude you desire. Then, *re-view* that past situation. Play it back in your mind in as much detail as possible. Re-view the actions, feelings, and thoughts that helped you be successful. Look for the little things you did, the gestures you used, the routines you set up, your movements, and your tone of voice.

Run your mental tape back to a point before the event and see how you psyched yourself up or calmed yourself down for it. Look at everything you did that might be helpful in this situation.

Then, see yourself accomplishing your goal, shaking hands with the client who signed the contract, finishing the project, being applauded by an appreciative audience. Seeing yourself achieve a past goal will help you to re-experience the feelings of confidence, exhilaration, and overall wellbeing that you had at that time.

Rerun your tape several times. Make your 'movie' as real as possible. Picture where you were, who was there, even what you were wearing. Everything. The impact of this past imagery on your present attitude and actions will increase in direct proportion to the clarity, detail, and intensity of your imagery.

## BRINGING THE PAST INTO THE FUTURE

The next step is to transfer your experience into the future. Preview an upcoming performance, see yourself performing with the same confidence, attitude, and skills in the upcoming situation that you had in the past one. Project into the future. Visualize yourself thinking, feeling, and acting in the Peak Zone with as much clarity and detail as possible. See the environment you will be in. Visualize yourself in action, being at your best accomplishing your goal.

Previewing will increase your confidence. You are also automatically practicing and refining your skills when using this mental rehearsal technique. Previewing also serves to make the real situation, when you are in it, seem more familiar which will make you more comfortable.

## PREVIEWING THE PERFECT PERFORMANCE

"I never hit a shot, not even in practice," says Jack Nicklaus, "without having a very sharp, in-focus picture of it in my mind. It's like a color movie. First, I see the ball where I want it to finish, nice and white, and sitting up high on the bright green grass. Then, the scene quickly changes and I see the ball going there—its path, trajectory, and shape, even its behavior on landing. Then, there is sort of a fade-out, and the next scene shows me making the kind of swing that will turn the previous images into reality."[7]

Tiger Woods's dad taught him, when putting, to visualize the ball's path to the hole and then "putt to the picture." Tiger makes the "picture" by standing halfway between the ball and the hole on the high side of the break and takes some short practice strokes from that spot, picturing how the ball will roll to the cup from there. Then, he goes back behind the ball and adds the first part of the read into his mental picture.[8]

Many top performers, such as Nicklaus and Tiger Woods, have images of when they were in the 'Peak Zone' already imprinted in their mind. Their best performances have been repeatedly grooved. When visualizing, they simply project those images into the future situation without needing to review an experience.

Scott T., the president of a marketing research company, was called on to testify at a highly publicized trial involving one of his firm's clients. Although all he had to do was present research data, which he did regularly at client meetings, he was worried about how he would come across. He was concerned that his nervousness might be construed as evasion and that he would lose his credibility. He also felt a lot of pressure because the client for whom he was testifying was a major one for his firm.

Scott prepared himself by previewing. He imagined himself calmly walking into the courtroom and sitting down. He saw all the details in the room—where he sat, with whom, the judge, the two sets of attorneys, his clients, the spectators. He then visualized himself being called to the witness stand and played out the scene, seeing himself at his best, responding to questions and presenting his research findings, speaking slowly and clearly making eye contact with the lawyer. Then, he saw himself leave the witness stand feeling confident and self-assured.

After several mental run-throughs, he was relaxed and feeling much more positive. He later said that testifying had been a snap. "I felt like I had been through the whole thing before. Funny, though, the scenario that I rehearsed in my head was a lot tougher than the real one."

## IDEAL MODELS

Bill Russell, the Hall-of-Fame center for the Boston Celtics, who revolutionized defensive play in basketball, used visualization as a teenager to practice new moves while traveling from one game to another on the high school bus. "I was in my own private basketball laboratory, making mental blueprints for myself. It was effortless; the movies I saw in my head seemed to have their own projector, and whenever I closed my eyes, it would run . . . As our tour rolled through a string of cities . . . I was not only learning the game, but adding to it. Every day turned into an adventure."[9]

Russell used an ideal model in his imagery to learn new skills and refine his moves. "I was working on learning how to take an offensive rebound and move quickly to the hoop. It's a fairly simple play for any big man in basketball, but I didn't execute it well, and McKelvey [another player] did. Since I had an accurate version of his technique in my head, I started playing with that image, running back the picture several times, and each time, inserting a part of me for McKelvey. Finally, I saw myself making the whole move, and I ran this over and over too. When I went into the game, I grabbed an offensive rebound and put it in the basket just the way McKelvey did. It seemed natural, almost as if I were just stepping into the film."[10]

Having an ideal model provides you with mental pictures that act as a guide for refining your own performance. You can use it to develop a specific attitude such as aggressiveness or receptiveness. Modeling involves watching someone whose style you would like to emulate or from whom you could learn specific skills that would improve your effectiveness. You can emulate the open-mindedness with which someone responds to suggestions, the authoritativeness with which someone runs a meeting, the determination of Marie Curie, the inspiration of Martin Luther King, the competitiveness of Bill Russell.

## JFK, COS, AND I

I used to watch comedians when I was getting started because trying to make people laugh, especially in comedy clubs where the audiences can be tough, isn't easy. As a result, a good comedian must have great timing, a terrific ability to tell a story, and be able to connect with an audience.

Watching comedians helped me to realize that there is no one right way to be good. There are as many different ways as there are people. Think about it—every good comedian has his or her own unique style. Look at the range: Chris Rock, Stephen Colbert, Jay Leno, Billy Crystal, Whoopi Goldberg, Richard Pryor, Joan Rivers, Eddie Izzard, and my current favorite, Jon Stewart. They're all terrific and all very different. The key is to find someone whose style you can identify with and then study him or her—not to copy, but to learn areas you want to improve such as timing, telling a story, and making contact with the audience.

But you don't have to have comedians as models. Pick anyone who is very good and who has a style you can identify with. Some presidents, such as Ronald Reagan, Bill Clinton, John F. Kennedy, and now, Barack Obama, have been great speakers, and of course, there was Martin Luther King, Jr. Or study people who are out on the speaking circuit. If you are smart, energetic, and controversial, you might try watching Tom Peters. If you are more of a techie, there's Daniel Burrus who is terrific speaking about the future of technology. But make sure that the person you are modeling is one with whom you have similar qualities. If you are more of an introvert and have a sly humor, don't pick Chris Rock as your model.

I used to spend many hours watching tapes of the young Bill Cosby playing the clubs. He had a wonderful ability to use his body with sound effects to tell tales of Fat Albert and the guys on the block. He also seemed to be having a lot of fun while telling his stories. Since I am an animated and high-energy speaker, I could relate to Cosby's style and learned a great deal from just watching him.

But don't pick someone just because you like him or her. To get the most out of this exercise, choose someone whose style or personality is closest to your own. It would be unwise for me to use Bob Newhart as a model because his style is so different from mine.

You can also pick someone who executes a certain skill you would like to develop or improve, as in the next examples.

When I began speaking to large audiences, I was intimidated and nervous. At about this time, I happened to view a film of John Kennedy giving his inaugural address. I was very moved by his presence and made it a point to review many of his speeches. I began developing a mental tape of him, seeing him in my mind's eye making a major speech. My mental picture of him focused on his power, authority, and presence. Gradually, I began replacing his image with mine until I could see myself as an authoritative speaker.

## IDEAL MODELING

To maximize your own performance by using an ideal model, first choose an individual who expresses those characteristics you want to develop, as I did with JFK and Cosby. Then, create a mental tape of examples of these characteristics so that you can see them clearly in your mind. Gradually edit yourself into the tape until you can see yourself performing with the same assurance as your model. With practice, this visualized behavior will become a natural response when you are in the real situation.

## TURNING FAILURE TO SUCCESS— EDITING YOUR TAPE

Several years ago, the governor of a large Midwestern state told me he had changed his relations with the press by using this technique. "When I was first elected, my relations with the press were very poor. I couldn't figure it out, since I knew that my stand on most of the issues was popular. I also knew I was well informed, so that couldn't have been the problem. I was puzzled and concerned. My wife suggested my problem might have less to do with what I said than how I said it. Her comment got me to review one of my press conferences on. videotape. Watching it, I realized that she was right. I was standing with my arms crossed; my mouth was tight; and I was hunched over. I looked very unfriendly, defensive, and angry. I didn't even like me.

"For my next meeting, in addition to preparing my remarks and information," the governor continued, "I visualized how I wanted to look, in terms of my posture, the expression on my face, and my movements. I also saw myself being more open and friendly and not as defensive. From that day on, my relations with the press improved dramatically."

"If I had a play that I muffed on the court, I'd go over it repeatedly in my head, searching for details I'd missed," said Bill Russell. "It was like working on a jigsaw puzzle; one piece in the completed picture was imperfect, and I had to find out what it was."[11]

The approach to mistakes is to "catch 'em and correct 'em." Errors not found tend to be repeated. The best time for this reviewing process is as soon as possible after the situation occurs.

The advantage of finding errors is that they can be corrected. Jean-Claude Killy, the former Olympic triple gold medal winner, used visualization, as many ski racers do, to prepare for his races. Before one race, it is said, Killy saw himself in his mental movie falling at a gate, something he rarely did. He reviewed the race in his mind and once again saw himself fall at the same gate. But this time, he discovered why. He had been skiing into that gate at too sharp an angle. He then reran the mental movie, seeing himself take a less extreme angle into that gate. It worked perfectly. He reran it several more times in his mind to get it perfect. The next day, he took the less extreme line at that gate and won the race.

You can use visualization to correct mistakes, break habits, and turn failure to success. You can edit your mental movie, replacing the error with pictures of yourself performing correctly. After editing your peak performance into the tape, re-view it often to imprint the changes in your mind. This new version will then become foremost in your memory and will be your automatic response to that situation.

## GUIDELINES FOR MAKING YOUR OWN MOVIES

Although *imagery* is the term most generally used for mental movies, not everyone sees pictures. Mental imagery is auditory, kinesthetic, and olfactory, as well as visual. Some people are more inclined or oriented toward one of these senses than the others. Many people who use visualization very effectively never "see" their mental movies. Some get a "feel" for the picture or "sense" it. A good friend of mine "listens" to it.

The following guidelines will help to make your mental movies more effective. Although we use the word *see* in these guidelines, it is meant to encompass any other ways you might experience your imagery.

1. *Relaxation.* You can't take a good picture if your camera isn't steady. Similarly, visualization is most effective if your mind is steady. The more relaxed and free of distraction you are when visualizing, the clearer your mental pictures will be, and the images will imprint more deeply.

2. *Make Them Real.* The effectiveness of your imagery is largely dependent on how specific and detailed it is. Your mental movie should be as close to the real thing as possible. If you are rehearsing for a meeting, for instance, start by seeing something familiar and build on it until you can see the scene fully. Take your time. Keep adding details until you have a sense of being there. Then, see yourself going through the same step-by-step sequence you would in the situation.

3. *Your Own Role in the Movie.* You can play two roles in your movie. You can play the observer and watch yourself perform, which is helpful when you are reviewing an experience or using an ideal model, as it allows you a more objective look at your performance.

   You can also play the participant—be the player in your own movie make it seem  as if you were in that situation, feeling what you would be feeling, seeing what you would be seeing.  Being the subject of your own movie is particularly useful when you are rehearsing for an upcoming situation.

   To get the greatest benefit from your mental movies, play both these roles. See how it looks from the outside, and then feel and practice it from the inside.

4. *Experience It Fully*. A friend told me that when Jean-Claude Killy visualized a ski race, he could hear the crowd, feel the wind and the cold on his face, and feel his legs pumping and the edges of his skis carving through the snow. Olympic track star Mary Decker experienced the feeling of coming off the final turn in the 3,000-meter run, lifting her knees and arms, extending her stride, sprinting fast. In the basketball foul-shooting experiment involving visualization, those who did best reported feeling the ball in their hands, feeling their knees bending as they shot, and hearing the swish as the ball went through the net. The Canadian heart patients, mentioned earlier, pictured themselves in a beautiful meadow filling their lungs with wonderful fresh air and feeling the oxygen going through the body and reaching the heart.[12]

Experiencing your mental movie as fully as you can imprints that ideal behavior image most effectively.

## TRIGGERS AND RITUALS

You can increase the effectiveness of your mental imagery by using a trigger or a ritual —a specific action transferred from your imagery into the real situation. A trigger serves as an "on" switch, automatically re-creating, in a situation, the behavior you rehearsed in your mental movie.

When you are developing your mental movie, select some action—such as taking a drink of water, polishing your glasses, turning your ring, holding your hands a certain way—that can be transferred to the real situation. Rerun that part of the movie. Practice the trigger physically as you are visualizing yourself doing it. These triggers help to bring that positive imagery to the forefront of your mind when in the real situation. These images will then guide your behavior in the situation.

Many professional athletes have specific rituals and even superstitions meant to help them to trigger a certain desired response. Former pro football star and best-selling author Dave Meggyesy told me that before every game, he would lace his shoes in a certain way. Tennis star Rafael Nadal must have exactly two water bottles at courtside. At each changeover, the bottles must be lined up so the labels face the end he is playing. Loren Ochoa, the former no.1 women's pro golfer, says she marked her ball with a coin on the green. Then, when she replaces the coin with the ball, she casually flips the coin into the air and catches it. "It's something that helps me relax and get it going."[13] San Francisco Giants star Pablo Sandoval makes a cross on the sand with his bat before entering the batter's box. It must work, since in his first full year in the majors, at the age of 22, his .330 batting average was the second best in the National League.

I have my own ritual before giving a speech. To be energized, I don my headphones about fifteen minutes prior to going on and listen to some rock music.

# PRACTICE ANYWHERE

Visualization is a powerful tool you can carry with you anywhere. You can practice it in your office, commuting, waiting in line, in elevators, before you go to bed, on vacations, and even as Joe Morgan did, in the bathtub. Rerunning a well-edited Peak Zone performance tape is exciting and exhilarating. It increases your confidence and prepares you to perform at your best.

# 13
# THE 90% SOLUTION

Nothing builds confidence like success. "Building success into your goals is critical," says Charles Lynch. "It's important to see success. Once you have succeeded, you can build on that. You can take another step up the ladder. These initially small successes build a sense of accomplishment." Success can be programmed into your action plan, building confidence, motivation and momentum.

In our Inner Skiing programs, we would often take skiers to a challenging run they hadn't previously skied, but which we knew they could do. Looking at the slope, they would often freeze. "You see that Black Diamond (the slope's designated difficulty level)! You know what that black stands for—**death**!" And as their panic grew, they'd suddenly "have to go to the bathroom" or needed "a cup of coffee."

I would then have them look at the slope. Where do you think they looked? All the way down to the bottom. The truth is that you can't see that far accurately, so as we have discussed, your fear-driven mind 'sees' snow snakes and mogul monsters. Four inch bumps look like they're four feet high.

I would then shift their gaze by asking them if they could see one turn they *could make.* "And make sure it is one you're sure you can do," I would tell them. I'd then have them take that one turn and stop.

"How are you feeling now?" I would ask. "A little better" would be the response.

I would then have them do the same exercise two or three more times, making sure each turn was a success. The change was dramatic. After three successful turns, their response invariably was, "Hey, this isn't as hard as I thought," and off they'd go down the slope. The three "can-do" turns had increased their confidence and their fear was replaced by excitement.

This idea of going for what you can do is key in any sport or anything you do, for that matter. Golfer Tom Watson, the number one player in the world from 1978 through 1982 and winner of eight major championships, said that a problem with most golfers is that they aim improperly. "They don't play the widest areas; they play into the riskiest areas."[1] And what happens when that that risky shot fails, just as when the skier falls while taking a turn he is not ready for--confidence plummets and enthusiasm gets deflated.

## START EACH DAY WITH A WIN

If you want to build confidence, start with a win, a "can-do." I always tell salespeople to try to schedule their first call of the day with one they are reasonably sure they will succeed, even if they have to go out of their way. If your first sales call or your first task is a win, it gets you pumped. Same is true with any project. Starting with a can-do will create confidence and momentum and overcome fear and procrastination.

The contract for my first book was for 50,000 words. I freaked! I'd never written much more than a two page article and that number, like the skier looking all the way down the slope, seemed impossible. Ever time I started to think about it, I'd suddenly have to have a cup of coffee or make a phone call. Finally, taking the advice I teach, I started to list the can-do's. First step-- enlarge the outline. No problem, I can do that. Second, write down a list of chapter headings. I can do that. Then start, not at the beginning, but with the chapter I knew I could do. Did that. By then I was on my way and eight months later I had finished.

Starting anything you are doing with a win increases your confidence and enthusiasm. And pretty soon you are on a roll.

## ON THE OTHER HAND

Consider if the skiers had tried a turn that was too difficult and fell. How do you think they'd have felt ? "See, I knew this was too hard" would be the response, and they'd quit or their fear and doubt would be reinforced. They'd then be overly tense on the next turn and lean back to prevent falling again. And as any skier knows, leaning back causes you to fall.

Same at work. If your first call or first task is a bummer, you become deflated. It takes the wind out of your sails. And what are you thinking about when making your next call? That 'damn' last one, so you won't do well on that one either. And the vicious cycle has started. Soon, you're ready to pack it in mentally, thinking it's not your day.

## THE 90% SOLUTION

My teachers and coaches always taught me to try to do a little more than I thought I could. Set your goals higher, I was told. Trying something that I thought was too difficult, would cause me to tense up, over try and land in the Panic Zone.

*My philosophy now is to try for a little less than you think you can do.* I'm not saying to try something that's a piece of cake and too easy. The intermediate skier on the beginners' slope ends up in the Drone Zone—bored, unmotivated and unfocused, and it goes downhill from there. Similarly, competing against someone whose ability is too far below yours, or a project that is too easy, decreases your motivation and concentration preventing you from playing your best game.

My approach is; go for something that is about 90% of what you think you can do. It should motivate and challenge, but not panic, you. That way, you'll stretch, but won't strain and try too hard—and you'll be successful. With a win or two under your belt, you'll then be more confident and motivated. Before long, the confidence built from some early wins will carry over into the day you'll end up doing more than you thought you could.

Remember to start everyday with a win. Can-do action steps dispel fear and create confidence and positive momentum.

# 14
## TRY EASIER

As a young athlete I was always taught by my coaches that if I wanted to excel and be a winner that 100% effort isn't enough. 'You've got to give 110%' one told me. But while working on my degree in sports psychology I read about the approach that Bud Winter, the San Jose State and U.S. Olympic track coach, used that caused me to rethink this "try harder" approach. Winter, who is now a member of the USATF Hall of Fame had coached gold medalists and world record holders like Lee Evans, Tommy Smith and Ray Norton. Noticing that the runners seemed overly tense and tight while trying to get that last ounce of speed, Winter told them to try running at 90%. The transition was amazing! Everyone had better times running at 90% effort then at 100 or 110%. I was amazed! The old 'give it everything you've got' approach didn't work as well as not giving it everything you've got."

I then began to notice that same thing in other sports. Think about a sport you play, for instance, when you are at your best in golf, hitting drives straight and far down the fairway. Doesn't it feel as if you *aren't* swinging as hard? Or when you're playing 'over your head' in tennis or flowing down a ski slope with ease and grace—doesn't it always feel easy, as if you weren't even trying? And the word many people use when describing their Peak Zone experiences, in all different types of situations, is 'effortless.'

## STRETCH, DON'T STRAIN

The problem with the 'try harder' approach is that when you push yourself to exceed what you think you can do, you will often tense up and try too hard. The result is you lose your rhythm, timing and flow and end up in the Panic Zone.

I was drawn to yoga more than twenty years ago when a herniated disc caused me to be bed ridden for a month. I have been practicing it ever since with remarkable results— no pain and increased flexibility. A basic premise of yoga is "stretch not strain." Trying to push your body beyond the stretch point into pain will invariably work against you, causing a pulled muscle or worse. This principle applies to every aspect of life and flies directly in the face of the false ideal, no pain, no gain!

## DON'T GO ALL OUT

Tom Telles, the coach of Olympic great Carl Lewis had Lewis running at 90%. Ray Evernham, the crew chief for Winston Cup winner, Jeff Gordon, says, "Sometimes, I'll tell him [Jeff] to go out and bust me a lap, and he'll drive the car hard, really work it, mash the pedal, drive down into a corner, jam the brakes, and mash the pedal again. Then, I'll say, 'Now, take it easy, and drive a smooth lap,' and he actually improves his time."[1]

Bruce Lee, the martial arts master, once said, "The less effort, the faster and more powerful you will be." Golfing great Sam Sneed said, "You can't swing slow enough." And former no. 1 women's golfer Annika Sorenstam says tempo is the first thing you lose when you try to overpower the ball. "I always remind myself to "swing 6" (at only 60% of my hardest swing)." Echoing Sneed, she says, "A slow swing will still create a powerful shot."[2] And Ernie Els says, "You'll get better results—and often more distance—if you swing at 80%."[3]

## TAKING THE GRUNT OUT

The career of former Brooklyn Dodger pitching great Sandy Koufax, named the athlete of the century by *Sports Illustrated*, hardly started out as a stepping stone to the Hall of Fame. After six years in the majors, his record was a paltry 36 wins and 40 losses. His problem was that though he had a blinding fastball, he was wild, and couldn't control it.

The turning point in his career came when he was scheduled to pitch the first half of a spring training game. When the pitcher scheduled for the second half missed his plane, Koufax volunteered to pitch the entire game. So he could last all nine innings, catcher Norm Sherry advised Koufax to ease up slightly on his fastball. The rest, as they say, is history. Koufax learned that a fastball would behave better with just as much life and better control if you throttle back a little. The result was that he pitched a no-hitter and said, "I came home a different pitcher from the one who had left."[4]

These days, when Koufax coaches young pitchers, he shares the lesson that took him six years to learn and saved his career. "Take the grunt out,"[5] he tells them.

## AND AT WORK

Koufax' wisdom works in any area of your life, from pitching a ball game or pitching a new client. Taking the grunt out, easing up on the throttle just a little, will enable you to be more relaxed, think more clearly, respond more appropriately, and perform at a peak level, no matter what you are doing.

Think about a time when you were at your best at work. It could have been when you were giving a presentation and had the group in the palm of your hands, handling a tough negotiation or customer problem with ease and style, or zipping through that pile on your desk. Isn't it true that when you are at the top of your game, whatever your game is, you are more relaxed, and it always feels easy, like 90% effort?

## SELLING EASY

Conventional wisdom in selling is to have salespeople make as many calls as possible. The thinking being that the more calls you make, the more sales you will get. Rather like the more times you are at bat, the more hits you are bound to make.

I have experimented with more than 150 sales groups, ranging from those making high-level executive calls to telemarketing. My approach is to have half the group make as many calls as they can. The other half is instructed to make fewer calls, to work at 90% effort.

In every instance, the group that made fewer calls had at least 20% better results. Why? "When I'm trying to make as many call as possible" a saleswoman who did detailing for a major pharmaceutical company told me, " I feel as though I'm racing inside and end up talking faster and not listening to anything besides the voice in my head telling me to hurry so I can keep on schedule. And then if I have to wait too long to see the doc, I'm really stressed which isn't a good mind set for talking to anyone."

The word that invariably comes up with the group that made fewer calls, but had more sales, was *quality* of the call. A typical response is; "I feel more relaxed and as a result I'm able to listen better, think more clearly and be a better problem solver for my client".

## SPEAK EASY

Early in my career as a speaker, when I felt a speech wasn't going well I would push harder. I'd begin to talk louder and faster, be more emphatic. But, I quickly discovered, this strategy only made things worse. The harder I pushed, the worse I would get, losing my timing, sense of humor and ultimately my connection with the group. This 'push harder' approach even caused me to forget some important points. After one of these performances, a friend told me that I seemed angry with the audience, which I probably was.

Now, when I sense a speech isn't going as well as I'd like, rather than push harder, I ease up which works much better. I'll talk a little slower, take a breath and look around to get a sense of what's going on. I've also found that when I'm more relaxed my sense of humor returns. As an example when an audience isn't responding to a question I'll sometimes say, in a tongue in check manner;" That is known as a question!" which usually evokes laughter and a lot of responses. And I'm back on track. To remind myself not to push I always write the word "Fun" on my speech notes. Yeah, even after 2000+ keynote speeches I sometimes need that little reminder

## WORK LESS

"In the final analysis workaholics are not business successes," says Patti Manuel, the former president and chief operating officer of Sprint's long distance division. "There are people at Sprint who work from sun up to well past sundown. They might make middle management, but then, they are stuck. They can't lift their heads above the trenches and... make horrible managers. I try to guard against that syndrome.

"I try and create an environment in which people get ahead because of their contribution, not because of the number of hours they log. I let people know that balance is important. I take off Wednesday afternoons to volunteer at my son's school. People who work too much have a massive amount of discipline, but they're not applying it in the right way."[6]

## PACING

Working at 110% will not only land you in the Panic Zone, it'll cause you to burn out or blow out. Jeffrey Miller, a former vice president at Intel and president and CEO of Documentum, advises his people " in order to prevent insanity, frustration, and burnout, people need to find their own pace. I learned this from my mentors at Intel," says Miller. "Each year, as I continued up the organization, I noticed I was working one hour longer. I also noticed that my mentor worked fewer hours than I did. I asked him what his secret was. He suggested figuring out a pace that I could keep up over the long term. I might have to sprint occasionally, but if I found the right overall pace, I'd be golden."[7]

Stewart Brand, whose 30-year history of pioneering achievement includes launching the legendary Whole Earth Catalogue, creating the New Games Tournament, and co-founding the Global Business Network, advises us that "If you want to keep speeding up, you'll also have to learn how to slow down."[8]

## NOT KICKING BACK

I'm not saying that if you simply kick back and do nothing, you'll get great results. Those 90%-effort sales groups still made many calls, and Carl Lewis didn't just go into cruise control on the track. But to excel, you need to take the panicked edge out of your efforts and stretch not strain. This shift will take you from the Panic Zone into the Challenge Zone.

My rule is that *A passionate 90% effort is more effective, productive, and creative than a panicked 110%. Stretch, don't strain.*

So, whether you're trying to drop a few strokes from your golf game or add to your numbers at work, remember to take the grunt out of your efforts and throttle back *just a little.* And the next time everything around you speeds up, *slow down.*

Learning to *Try Easier* will not only improve your performance and creativity, but the quality of your life. I have a sign on my desk that says 90% and a vanity license plate that reads TRY EZR to remind me of this message, which is so counter to most of what I learned in the past.

# 15
# TURNING FAILURE INTO SUCCESS

At a conference I attended, Walter Wriston, then chairman of Citicorp, said, "Failure is not a crime; failure to learn from failure is...."[1] How much and how fast we learn, not how many or how few mistakes we make, determine the difference between the "best" and the rest of us.

To keep ahead of today's challenges, you must be innovative and creative, which means taking risks and trying things not done before. As a result, you'll inevitably make some mistakes. You can't try things you haven't done before and expect to get it right the first time. That'd be like a first time skier expecting not to fall. It's therefore not *if* you make mistakes, but *what* you do *after* you make them that determines how well you will do.

# TO ERR IS TO LEARN

Mistakes are inevitable. The real problem is that we often don't automatically learn from them, so we end up repeating them. Most of us, after a mistake, failure, or error, think, "Well, I won't make that mistake again." But resolving not to make the same mistake again doesn't work. You have to know what caused it to correct it. One problem is that we often fail to look closely at our mistakes because we attach a stigma to errors. We believe that we should know how to "do it right the first time." This is especially a problem for bright, well-educated people who are used to being rewarded for being "right."

Early in life, most of us found out that mistakes can be painful. Parents and teachers didn't praise us for mistakes. Quite the opposite—our mistakes were often faulted in front of the class, causing us feel foolish, humiliated, and embarrassed. These early experiences often affect our behavior for a lifetime.

Since no one wants to appear foolish or think of him9 or herself as stupid, we often go to great lengths to avoid *admitting* we made a mistake, even to ourselves. This response blocks the objectivity needed to learn and bounce back. Here are some defensive ways in which we respond after making a mistake.

## NOT ME

One of the toughest defenses to dismantle is denial, because it's so hard to catch. Denial is a habit that starts early when a kid who has been criticized too much learns to duck first and ask questions later... or maybe never.

When you deny you made a mistake, you fail to accept responsibility for it. As a result you wind up lying to yourself, distorting the facts about even small errors, making it impossible to learn from, since you can't learn from something that you aren't willing to look at.

Peter Parker, the former head of British Railways, said, "The most difficult person in management is the mistake concealer. If someone walks into my office saying, 'I screwed up,' I say, 'Come in.' In the healthiest organizations, the taboo is not on making mistakes, but on concealing them."[2]

"Having a positive attitude towards mistakes allows them to be corrected rapidly when they occur," adds Monty Python's John Cleese, a successful businessman and film producer in his own right. "The problems come when mistakes are denied," says Cleese. "If we don't acknowledge a mistake, we can't very well correct it."[3]

## COVER IT UP

If you view mistakes as bad and failure as frightening, then failure and discovery are catastrophic. Consequently, people will go to great lengths to avoid being perceived as a failure or to admit a mistake ever happened. To cover up mistakes, they try to hide the truth and hope no one will notice.

In his best-selling book, *Swim with the Sharks Without Being Eaten Alive*, Harvey Mackay wrote; "Stubbornness in refusing to recognize a problem has destroyed a lot of the bottom lines... You can't solve a problem unless you first admit you have one."[4]

Cover-ups take a lot of energy. Often, the defensive, elaborate disguises become so intricate and complex that they end up having a life of their own. To cover up usually requires a labyrinth of supporting lies to shore up the original "big" one. A cover-up uses all the creative juice you could have used to learn from the original mistake—and fix it.

A classic example was the incredible chain of events that began with the White House-sanctioned break-ins at the Watergate complex. The early denials and the ensuing cover-ups became much more of a problem than the initial mistake. Eventually, exposing the elaborate cover-up led to the resignation of President Richard Nixon.

*Deny a mistake, and you deny yourself the chance to learn from it.*

## POINTING THE FINGER

Blaming occurs when a mistake is so obvious you can't deny it, so you try the next best thing—pointing a finger at someone else, "not my fault!" The boss blames the staff; marketing blames research and development; the teacher blames the principal. The blamer tries to put everyone else on the hook.

Consider the golfer who tenses up, swings too hard and hits a drive into the rough. And who then blames the course's narrow fairways, his clubs, other people talking, the wind... He is willing to blame anything rather than admit an error. Sounds familiar, doesn't it? We do it all the time. We blame the client for not buying, the boss for not listening, the audience for not clapping, and the baby for not eating.

Turnaround specialist Timothy Finley said about a company he bought, that he found the president "pointed the finger of blame at the sales manager for the lack of profitability, and the sales manager pointed the finger of blame at the president." Looking at the facts objectively, Finley discovered that both had made mistakes. But each was so busy passing the buck that there was "too much blaming and not much learning."[5]

Blaming others is tempting to escape the consequences. But when you blame a mistake on others—be it your boss, your customers, or your kids—you deprive yourself of an opportunity to learn. And you can be sure the error will be repeated. Soon you won't have anyone or anything left to blame

## ANGER!

Who hasn't seen (or been) the tennis player who smashes her racquet on the ground after a bad shot; the skier who, after a fall, whips the snow with his poles; or the executive who pounds on the desk after a bad phone call or meeting? Fury and anger are very common responses when we make a mistake. They are such intense emotions that they overpower you and those around you. Sometimes, the anger is "other-directed" and often irrationally used to attack others. But most often, we direct it inside, as we assault our own self-esteem with both fists. 'I'm so stupid, how could I have done that!!'

Anger leaves emotional bumps, bruises, and scars, which prevent you from thinking clearly and rationally. When still smoldering it prevents you from getting back into the "game." The golfer, still angry with himself for missing a putt, is now tense as he stands at the next tee. Upset and tight, he overswings, turning a bad putt into a bad drive and a bad drive into a triple-digit round!

Similarly, the manager, angry with herself for making a mistake in a meeting or on the phone to a client, doesn't calm down and focus on the next task. The next thing you know, the phone rings, and she vents her anger on the next caller.

## DAMN! I DID IT AGAIN!

While avoidance and denial skirt the issue, and blame flings it at others, another mistake we make is to point the finger at ourselves. We rehash an error ad infinitum, beating ourselves into the ground. We run the "Damn! I did it again!" tape over and over. Frequently, a baseball pitcher will give up a homerun and then often have the following batter hit another homer. Guess what he was thinking about when facing that next batter.

Dwelling on our mistakes is a way of replaying a mental failure tape. The more you ruminate on the mistake, the more deeply it becomes etched in your mind and magnified out of proportion. The next time you face a similar situation, up pops the past failure tape from your memory bank, and you think, "Uh oh, here I go again," and you're on to creating a vicious cycle.

# "SHAKE IT OFF"

At the other end of the spectrum is letting things go too quickly. During a recent softball game, our third baseman made an error on his throw to first. "Shake it off; forget about it," he was told. "Don't think about it. Concentrate on the next batter." He nodded and turned toward the batter's box. Next inning, he cleanly fielded a hard grounder and threw it over the first baseman's head, *again*. He had repeated the mistake because he hadn't stopped to realize that he was throwing off his back foot, causing his throws to sail over the head of the first baseman.

What "shake if off" means is don't get down on yourself. But this good advice all too often,  causes us to neglect learning what caused the error and how we could correct it. After a bad hit, you often see professional tennis players and golfers take a few imaginary practice swings to correct the mistake and get back in the "groove." If you move on without reflecting on what you did, or if you avoid facing the problem, chances are you will repeat it.

In the words of the immortal Spanish philosopher George Santayana, "Those who cannot remember the past are condemned to repeat it."

## WHAT YOU "CAN-DO' AFTER A MISTAKE

Below are four active steps to take to ensure that your mistakes become stepping stones. These Four *R's*—Admit *Re*-sponsibility; *Re*-view; *Re*-place; *Re*-hearse—will not only prevent you from repeating the same mistake, but will enable you to learn, grow, and turn past failures into successes.

## R1—ADMIT RE-SPONSIBILITY

Start by acknowledging your role in the situation, which gives you real power to effect change. A study of 191 top executives at *Fortune 500* companies indicated that virtually all had suffered "hardship experiences" ranging from missed promotions to firings to business failures. The survey conducted by the Center for Creative Leadership found that the executives who bounced back did so *"because instead of blaming others, they were able to admit their failures, and then move on."* They could analyze effectively and then learn from what happened. A good scientist doesn't worry or try to cover up for experiment that didn't go exactly as planned. Instead, he becomes curious about the reason it didn't work. This learning can often lead to a breakthrough.

Professional basketball or football players, after a bad throw, a dropped pass, or any miscue, will immediately accept responsibility. They'll say "My Bad," or you'll see them point to themselves.

Admitting a mistake, rather than avoiding it, denying it, blaming others, or any other defensive maneuver, helps you to see more clearly and have a better understanding of what caused it, which is the first step to preventing a repeat performance.

# R2—*RE*-VIEW YOUR SCRIPT

After you've made a mistake, go back in your mind, and *re-view* the situation as if you had a mental videotape in your head. *Rerun* the tape from start to finish to see the entire process. In the case of a bad decision, start the tape with the information you had and your research. Run through your entire decision process and then go to the meeting itself and "watch" it through to the end. As you review, find the point or points where you went astray and what you would change the next time. Was your information complete? Were you in too much of a hurry? Did you wait too long? Did you miss picking up on something the client said? Were you too worried about the cost? Be as specific as possible.

Thoughts precede actions. Once you isolate the behavior that didn't work, find out what you were thinking at that moment. The golfer's over-swing made him shank the drive; but the thought "I've gotta hit the cover off the ball" created the over-swing. Or, it could have been an attitude or an emotion. A "play-it-safe" attitude might have caused you to delay making the decision. Or the 'gottas' might have caused you to move too quickly, without looking at all the information.

The key in a *re*-view is to look at both your behavior and the thought that led to it. Focus on the point where you made the mistake, and then identify your thinking and the assumptions that created it.

# R3—*RE*-PLACE THE OLD FOOTAGE

It's not enough just to flag the error. To ensure you don't make the same mistake again, develop an alternative response so that the next time a similar situation develops, you're ready. Learn to replace the old picture with a better one. When you "edit" the "mistake" footage out of your mental tape and re-place it with something better, you're "splicing" in thoughts and actions that will help you to respond better the next time.

When I feel I haven't responded well to a question in a Q&A session after a speech, I will re-view the situation and develop a better response. I will then visualize the same question being asked and see myself responding in that new way. This step helps me to feel more confident and ready if that same question comes up.

After developing this new response, I can't guarantee that the re-edited version will ensure that I'm great in the next Q&A, but it helps me feel more confident, which is a big step in performing well in any situation.

# R4—*RE*-HEARSE THE NEW MOVES

The last step in the cycle is to mentally rehearse the new success tape. Rehearsing the "*re*-edited" tape imprints it in your mind, which helps it to become a natural response when the same type of situation occurs. Consequently, rather than repeating a mistake, you will have imprinted a more desirable response to the situation.

# TEACHING THE FOUR R'S
# TO URBAN HIGH SCHOOL

One of the most rewarding experiences of performance coaching I ever had was with San Francisco's Urban High School volleyball team, which my son Otis played for. Urban was the lowest-ranked team in the playoffs. Though they lacked experience (this being only the second year the school had a team) and had a height disadvantage, their worst problem was a mental one.

In a session before the playoffs, I discussed the above four R's, and the players realized that one of their problems regarding errors wasn't physical, but mental. They confessed that when one of them missed a spike, a set, or a pass, the rest of the team would get on his case—glaring at him; yelling, "wake up!"; and blaming him for not being positioned right- responses that caused that player to get down on himself. Some players also described how they'd get down on themselves after an error and lose concentration for the next few points.

We then explored ways to replace these negative responses. I asked, "What could you do differently when someone makes a mistake?" One player said, "We have to respect each other." Another said, "Yeah, we have to make each other feel good, not bad, after a mistake. You feel bad enough already."

I then had them mentally rehearse these positive responses and encouraged the team to visualize them that evening and before the next game. It was an inspiring session and everyone left feeling better, but the real surprise came the next day at the first playoff game. After one of our players blew a set, the rest all ran over and gave him a "high five" and some encouraging words. The same thing happened when the team's big hitter muffed one. Normally, he would get down on himself. This time, though, he cracked a little smile, quickly practiced a better move, and got right back into the game. Meanwhile, the opposition seemed to unravel, as Urban's players became more and more upbeat. The entire tournament went that way—they beat teams that were, on paper, far superior to them.

But the real test awaited them in the finals, a rematch with a much larger school that had slaughtered them in an earlier meeting. We won the first game, lost the second, won the third, and lost the fourth. It was so tense; you could taste the pressure. In the last game, as the lead went back and forth, the Urban team never lost its cool. The kids encouraged each other and kept their spirits up. Their opponents, though, became increasingly tense, frustrated, and agitated. Finally, with the game in overtime, as in a Hollywood movie, undersized and under-skilled Urban won. It was the school's first championship in any sport, and the team knew it wasn't luck. They had developed a new set of mental muscles allowing them the flexibility to make mistakes and, as winners in all fields, the resiliency to bounce back stronger. It helps to remember that *in every failure exists the seed of a new learning and a new opportunity.*

# 16
# FOCUSED CONCENTRATION— THE MASTER SKILL

I always asked with the Olympic athletes and teams I worked with, what the difference was between those who won medals and those who didn't. Their responses surprised me. They never mentioned ability or skills. "Everybody's got the skills, "or they wouldn't have made the team." I was told.   The quality most often mentioned was concentration or focus. It was the ability to focus on what they were doing and  block out everything else. Speaking of  the intense focus that Olympic gold medalist Phil Mahre had prior to a race, a member of the U.S. ski team told me , "He was in a cocoon of concentration, totally focused. You could almost feel it, and you didn't want to try and break it by talking to him."

Home-run king Hank Aaron is to have said that sometimes the ball seemed like a grapefruit and sometimes like an aspirin. The difference was the quality of his concentration.

I recently went to the President's Cup tournament in which the best golfers in the world were competing. At one hole, I stood in the first row. As the players arrived to tee off, people shouted out things like; "How's the knee, Ernie?" and "C'mon, VJ." But these athletes seemed to be in their own little world and didn't appear to hear or notice anything.

And when asked what he attributed to his being at his best under the intense pressure he faces, Tiger Woods, said "concentration....I get so enthralled in the moment that the subconscious takes over... And in those times, I don't hear noise, don't hear anything.[1] When you're over that putt, all you think about is where you're playing that ball. All the other stuff takes care of itself. It's nothing else but starting the ball on that line with the correct speed. That's it."[2]

## YOU MUST BE PRESENT TO WIN

The N.Y. Yankees' A-Rod, a three-time American League MVP and twelve-time all star, is one of the best baseball play-ers on the planet. When asked what his goals were for the upcoming season, I expected he would say something like; "to drive in more runs, hit more homers or raise my batting average." Instead, his response was "My only goal is to learn how to play one entire game in the present."

The immortal Bobby Jones, one of the greatest golfers in

history, echoing A-Rod's thinking, once said, "It's nothing new or original to say that golf is played one stroke at a time. But it took me years to realize it."[3]

The importance of focused concentration for peak performance isn't only true in sports, but in everything you do. The more focused you are when trying to solve a difficult problem, without distracting thoughts such as worrying about failing or where you're going later, the more clearly you can think and the more easily a solution is found.

"Most successful people have a phenomenal ability to consciously focus their attention," writes *NY Times* columnist and *PBS NewsHour* commentator David Brooks. "Control of attention is the ultimate individual power. It leads to self-control, the ability to formulate strategies in order to resist impulses. It leads to resilience, the ability to persevere with an idea, even when all the influences say it can't be done. It leads to creativity. Individuals who can focus attention have the ability to hold a subject or problem in their mind long enough to see it anew. We know from experiments with subjects as diverse as obsessive-compulsive disorders and Buddhist monks that people who can self-consciously focus their attention have the power to rewire their brains."[4]

## ABSORPTION

The type of concentration that gets you into that Peak Zone is a total absorption on what you are doing. At these times, your mind isn't wandering, flitting, and flighting around. You can see a great example of that by watching children at play or a cat waiting for a mouse. This type of concentration is like turning a 1,000-watt bulb shining in all directions into a beam of light completely honed in on the target. When the diffused light becomes a focused beam, we greatly increase our awareness in the single direction the ray is shining. Concentration is simply the process of focusing the light, of turning the beam into a laser-like ray.

The light of our awareness dims when our mind wanders. If we're thinking about how good we look, while skiing, or the après ski party we're going to, or any number of things, our attention is scattered. With our thoughts bouncing around, awareness of our body, skis, and terrain is greatly diminished as is our performance., We found that skiers often fell or made off balance turns, not because they didn't have the skills but because their attention was distracted, and they were thinking about things other than their skiing.

*Ultimately, your performance level directly relates to your concentration level.*

## PANIC AND DRONE ZONE CONCENTRATION

Being in the Panic Zone, scared or worried, before a presentation or other pressure situation, is like shaking that light so you don't see or think clearly. The focus of the scared speaker jumps from one thought to another, not seeming to focus on anything or any one person for more than a fleeting moment. The result of his scattered concentration is that he talks and moves too fast, doesn't think clearly and loses concentration with his audience. At these times even the well prepared, but nervous, speaker can forget important points and make mistakes.

If, when under the gun to finish a proposal, your mind starts wandering to; "I gotta get this finished by...; What if they don't buy it," "I wonder what my competition is going to offer," "This damn computer isn't fast enough," your concentration light is diffused. And you won't think as clearly or work as quickly and efficiently.

It's just the opposite when you are in the Drone Zone. We have all seen actors "phoning in" a performance or speakers giving a canned presentation that they have done a hundred times and just seem to be going through the motions with no enthusiasm or energy. Similarly a task is boring causes your mind to wander, resulting in mistakes and shoddy work. Being in the Drone Zone dims that focused light from 1000 watts to about 200.

## MOMENTARY DISTRACTIONS

An example of how easy and quickly your attention can be distracted and your performance derailed, happened to me when I was swimming in a meet in which the top two places could lead to the Olympic trials. I was totally focused for the first three laps and felt great. On the last turn I glanced quickly to see where I was. I was first! And the thought that flashed through my mind was; "I'm going to the Olympics!" That momentary loss of concentration caused me the lead and I came in third by .05 of a second. That's how quickly and subtly your mind can distract you.

A lapse of concentration, like mine, can happen at anytime in any type of situation. I have often noticed this type of distraction when I am giving a speech and I see a guy looking at his watch. My mind then immediately jumps from what I am talking about to; "Uh-oh, they're bored", which causes me to lose concentration, tighten up and start talking faster and louder .

The same type of distraction can also occur when things are going really well. At these times your mind, as mine did in that swimming race, can jump to; "I'm really doing great!" causing you to relax and lose your edge

Any type of momentary distraction such as these can cause you to lose focus. The key is to catch yourself quickly when this happens and refocus your attention on what you are doing. It's like retuning your radio when it slips off the station.

## CONCENTRATE—DAMN IT!

But often, when people lose focus and start making errors, they begin telling themselves to *"concentrate, damn it"* which never works, because now they're angry and are now focused on the "damn it" rather than on what they are doing. With the anger comes tension, a tight jaw, and over trying. The angry golfer swings too "damn hard," and the skier who just fell now has a death grip on his poles and is stabbing the snow as if it were the enemy. The result is their performance goes down-hill, which then causes them to get even angrier.

# THE DRUNKEN MONKEY

Speaking about performance under pressure, Tiger Woods says, *"The mind controls the body... It's a matter of getting the mind under control."*[5]

Sounds easy to concentrate on what you are doing, doesn't it? But can you consciously control where your attention goes? Can you consciously decide to keep your attention on the present moment and have your mind happily obey? Or does your mind seem to have a will of its own? Controlling the mind is perhaps the most difficult task any of us will ever face. Buddhist monks spend a lifetime pursuing this goal. Eastern philosopher and guru Ram Das, the former Dr Richard Alpert, once said that the mind is like a drunken monkey, dancing and jumping around at whatever attracts it at the moment. The only difference is that the mind flits from one thing to the next with a speed that even the fastest drunken monkey couldn't match.

# MENTAL PRACTICE

It's near impossible to stay focused on a single object for a single day, or even, much more than five minutes. To get an idea of how difficult it is to sustain focus , try this exercise;

*Take five minutes, and see if you can keep your focus on your breathing without having your mind flit around with thoughts, such as "What am I doing this for?", "This is boring," "Is the five minutes up yet?" Or even; " Hey I'm really getting this now"...or the myriad other thoughts that dance into your mind. To help keep your focus, you might count your breaths or inhale to the count of five and exhale to the count of six.. Or try to imagine you are watching your thoughts go by as if on a movie screen or radio. You will be amazed at the plethora of thoughts that will dance through your head in just five minutes. And that's when you are trying to concentrate!*

The mind, as any muscle, needs practice and work to grow. Olympic decathlon winner Bruce Jenner advises, *"You must train your mind like you train your body."*[6] Meditation is one way to practice mental focus, as are most of the Eastern martial arts and yoga. Central to each of these is the sustained focus on the present.

It's important to remember not to get mad at yourself when your mind wanders, because it will. Getting angry like that, as has been mentioned, just further distracts your attention from the present. Now, you are not only not concentrating, but the anger has made you tense and stressed as well. Training the mind is like teaching a wild animal—if you punish it for not obeying you, it will turn on you.[7] Get it through your head that your mind will wander, and when it does, gently bring it back to the present on what it is that you want to focus.

Everything that takes you out of the present moment is a distraction that interferes with the level of your concentration. Fear, for instance, jerks you into the future causing you to be anxious about something that hasn't happened. And there are the; " If only I had… ( said this or done that) which shifts your attention from where you *are now* to where you *were then.* Some distractions are very subtle and even pleasant such as having your mind drift off into some anticipated pleasurable future or a great past experience. But even the most pleasant distraction is still a distraction reducing the light of awareness.

## MENTAL BREAKS

It's easy to concentrate when reading a good book or watching an exciting movie or sporting event. Other times, such as when writing an involved proposal or trying to solve a complex problem, it's difficult. I have found, however, that whether you are concentrating on something enjoyable or difficult, your mind, as any muscle, gets tired and needs a break from the intensity. Friends and I record football and baseball games, so we can eliminate the commercial breaks. Sure, the game goes by faster, but without a break, we are as exhausted as the players at the end of the game.

When you're tired, your mind starts to wander, making it difficult to focus. My general rule, when writing, which is very demanding of my concentration, is that after an hour, I take a break, stretch, get a cup of coffee, take a little walk, doing something to relax my brain for a couple of minutes. Interestingly enough, I often get a new idea on these breaks. But whether I do or not, I come back from little breaks feeling more refreshed.

When my wife Marilyn and I were brainstorming while writing our book, *The C Zone* , she would often say, "I need a little nap." This, of course, drove the workaholic, pusher part of me crazy. "Nap! We've got to get this done!" I would say.

But she prevailed, and after a 10-minute nap, awakened more refreshed and often with a new perspective.

## YOU MUST BE PRESENT TO WIN

The key to performing in the Peak Zone is to learn how to focus your attention entirely on the present moment. It's like the saying; *'You have to be present to win'*. Many books, programs, seminars, and disciplines focus on learning to control your attention. The focus of the yogas, Zen, and martial arts such as Tai Chi, Aikido, Judo, and Karate is on quieting the mind and creating laser like concentration. The *Inner Game* books teach techniques for increasing awareness in sports such as tennis, golf, and skiing, and even music. When you are more 'in the moment', the moment seems to stretch, and you see more, think more clearly, and respond more appropriately.

Former San Francisco 49er All-Pro quarterback John Brodie talks about the ultimate experience of being entirely in the present moment. "A player's effectiveness is directly related to his ability to be right there, doing that thing in the moment. He can't be worrying about the past or future or the crowd or some other extraneous event." And in those intense moments of concentration, Brodie claims "time seems to slow way down, in an uncanny way, as if everyone were moving in slow motion. It seems as if I had all the time in the world to watch the receivers run their patterns, and yet, I know the defensive line is coming at me as fast as ever. I know perfectly well how hard and fast those guys are coming, and yet, the whole thing seems like a movie or a dance in slow motion."[8]

# 17

# GAINING CONTROL

Everybody acts. We are all busy doing something. But there's one basic difference between the way you focus when you're in the Peak Zone and when you're in the Panic or Drone Zone. That difference is control. In every situation, there are elements you can and can't control. Knowing the difference is critical. Focusing attention and acting on what you can control will maximize your performance and effectiveness. We often sabotage ourselves, however, by concentrating on factors outside our control, which skews our concentration and creates stress, frustration, and disappointment.

## CONTROL WHAT YOU CAN

Several years ago, Minnesota Twins outfielder Roger Ward was in a slump, hitting .226, when legendary coach Karl Kuehl asked him what he would be concentrating on in the game that night. "I want to get a couple of hits and drive in a couple of runs," was Ward's response.

"A hitter doesn't have any control over whether he gets any hits or drives in runs," Kuehl told him. "There might not be runners on base, so there'd be no one to drive in. A pitcher might make a perfect pitch. A fielder might make a great play. What a player *can control* is making sure he sees the ball well every time he goes up, making sure every swing he takes is a good one, making sure he knows the pitcher he is facing."[1]

Following Kuehl's advice and concentrating on what he could control, Ward went on a streak that saw him hit .326 with 22 home runs and 74 RBIs in the final 96 games of the season.

Ward's problem, common to many struggling to get out of a slump, was that he focused on factors that were out of his control. Every situation has a number of factors that influence the outcome. Some of these are in your control, and some aren't. Focusing on things out of your control is frustrating, and stress producing, and ensures Panic Zone or Drone Zone performance.

## WHAT YOU CAN AND CAN'T CONTROL

Something is not in your control if it is externally influenced. As Kuehl pointed out, if you are a batter, the pitchers performance and whether a fielder makes a great play are out of your control. Whether you win a game is also out of your control. You can control how well you play, but that's only one variable deciding the outcome. Another is how well your opponent and teammates play. And those are out of your control.

In a sales presentation for instance, you can't control the client's needs, attitude, or response; what the competition might have offered; or the state of the economy—all of which are significant factors in determining whether succeed or not. You can control the information you have about your client and the situation, and how you organize and present your material. Ultimately, whether you make the sale is out of your control.

## THE ECONOMY

The tendency to focus on things out of your control is especially true in a down economy. Tom Tierney, a senior V.P. of sales for American Express, says, "When things slow down, people tend to get paralyzed (because) they focus on what's not controllable like interest rates and the economy."[2]

Many of my clients tell me their people are worried about keeping their job, because of all the layoffs, the stock price which has been plummeting, the competition's new offerings. The resulting high levels of anxiety hinders their motivation as well as the quality of their work and life. Focusing on these issues however not only propels stress levels though the roof but is a huge waste of time and energy. Ultimately they have *no control* over the stock price, whether they are laid off, and what the competition is offering. What they *can control* is how motivated, productive and creative they are, which will hopefully influence management and prevent them from being laid off.

# THE PAST IS GONE

We've all been in situations in which we've said or done something we later regretted. To make things worse, long after such an incident, we obsess on our mistake, causing feelings of guilt, anger and worry about repercussions. If we don't blame ourselves for the past behavior or mistake, we blame someone else. Blame, worry, guilt, and anger shift our attention from the present.

You can't do anything to change the past. Past events, like future goals, are out of your control. You can learn from the past and, on the basis of that information, act in the present.

Speaking of letting go of the past, Loren Ochoa, the former no. 1 woman golfer in the world says, "I'm very good at just leaving things behind. I think that's important. A lot of players regret too much or get upset or angry (about past shots) and waste maybe one or two days of weeks being down. I'm easy with me. I do get really mad and disappointed, but I move on and leave things behind and put them in the trash can, and I keep going."[3]

# CONTROL AND INFLUENCE

Not only can you not control the economy; the past; or another person's needs, attitudes, responses or how well he plays a game; you can't ultimately control *anything* outside your own beliefs, attitudes, and actions. You, however, can influence a person's or company's actions, but influence is often a long way from control.

Performance Under Pressure

Larry Wilson, the co-author of the One Minute Sales Person, and founder and chairman of Wilson Learning Corporation a large management training company, and the Pecos River Learning Center, clarified this distinction between controlling and influencing others in the following way. In a wellness seminar we led, he pointed his finger at the audience and said, "If this were a gun and I told nobody to move, would I be in control of you?"

"Damn right!" was the first reply.

"Seriously," Larry said, "is this gun actually controlling your movements?"

"No, but it sure is a good influencer," someone shouted out.

"Right," Larry said, "and there is the difference. I can influence you in any number of ways, but ultimately I can't control what you do, even with this gun. Someone in the back could crawl out while I was looking the other way. Some other daring individual could throw something at me. Another person who didn't believe that I would shoot might call my bluff and just get out of her seat."

This might sound like double talk, but the best way to influence others and any external situation is to focus on what you can control, your attitude, behavior, and how well you listen and respond.

## DON'T WASTE YOUR ATTENTION

No matter how much you feel in control of a situation, if the outcome involves another person's actions or decisions, the result is out of your control. Great athletes seem to know this. They don't dwell on things they can't control. Julius Erving, the great Dr. J., had led his team to the National Basketball Association finals three times, but they lost each time. Yet, he said of this quest, "I don't feel incomplete or inadequate in any way because I haven't won an NBA championship. I don't lie awake nights and think about it. I know I've given my best. The rest is out of my hands."[4] Eventually Dr J and this then team did win the NBA Championship

When trade rumors abounded about former Cy Young Award winning pitcher and six-time All-Star Roy Halliday, he said it wasn't a distraction. Speaking of the possible trade and all the rumors, Halliday said, "It's nothing I can control, and I'm not going to worry about it."[5]

Despite the fact that three of his superstars defected to another league and a number of his star players were injured, Don Shula's Miami Dolphins won 2 Super Bowls, 5 AFC championships and were division winners 11 times. "I don't dwell on things I can't control," said Shula, a four time NFL coach of the year; "What's past is past. It's gone. It's yesterday."[6]

"You can't say you're going to win and then win," said Peter Carruthers who, with his sister, won a silver Olympic medal in pairs skating. "Kitty and I didn't come here to win a medal. We came to do the best we could. We can't control how the other skaters skate. We can't control how the judges mark us. All we can control is ourselves and our skating."[7]

# GOOD ADVICE

When I was behind in racquetball, I would often start yelling at myself: "Relax!" "Concentrate!" "Get those next three points!" "Keep on your toes!" I began noticing that some of these commands helped me play better, but most didn't.

The problem with much of the "good advice" I gave myself was that it didn't translate into action. What does "relax" mean? Which muscle? How much? I don't want to be too relaxed. "Concentrate!" On what? "Get those three points!" Sure, but how? What do you think I've been trying to do?

Because these commands weren't actionable they weren't much use and only served to increase the pressure I was putting on myself and fuel my Panic Zone performance. The advice that did work and improved my performance— "Keep on your toes," "Breathe out with every shot," "Keep moving all the time"—led me to take action that was specific, constructive, and in my control.

I applied these same parameters when I began giving keynote speeches and presentations. I had tried to counter my tendency to talk too fast by telling myself to speak slowly. I even wrote notes at the top of the pages of a speech telling me "Slow down!" But it didn't work. The problem was that "Slow down" wasn't specific enough. How slow? Like a 76RPM vinyl played at 33? The instructions were too ambiguous. Besides, I was usually in so much of a hurry that I forgot to look at the note. The instructions that did work were more specific and actionable; 'stop and take a breath after each point I had underlined as important, and make eye contact with three people in different parts of the room.' To perform in the Peak Zone more often focus on factors that are in your control, specific and actionable.

## DON'T FOCUS ON YOUR GOALS

When former Secretary of State and Chairman of the Joint Chiefs of Staff Colin Powell was a young second lieutenant, he asked an old general, "How do I become a general?" The general responded, "Son, you've got to work like a dog. You've got to have moral and physical courage. There may be days you feel tired, but you must never show fatigue. You'll be afraid, but you can never show fear. You must always be the leader."

"Thank you, sir. So, that's the key to becoming a general? said Powell.

"No," said the general, "that's how you become a first lieutenant, and then you keep doing it over and over."

"Throughout my career," said Powell, "I've always tried to do my best today. Think about tomorrow, and maybe dream a bit about the future, but doing your best in the present has to be the rule. You won't become a general unless you become a good first lieutenant."[8]

This is true about focusing on any kind of goal. "I don't want to think about it," said Tamara McKinney about winning the World Cup in skiing. "I got into trouble last month [she fell in three races] because I was thinking about winning it and putting too much pressure on myself. All I want to do is concentrate on each race."[9] With this new focus, McKinney, a few months later, became the first American woman to win the World Cup.

Performance Under Pressure

Focusing on the score in a game is another way we distract ourselves and make mistakes in the present. If you're skiing and concentrating on a mogul 10 feet ahead, you'll often blow it on the turn you are making. When faced with a five foot putt, thinking, "If I make this putt, I'll beat my handicap," invariably you'll miss it .

The same is true when making a big presentation. If you're focused on making the sale in a client meeting, you're attention is distracted and you you'll miss cues and clues from the group and probably forget important points. You'll also probably push too hard, talk too much, too fast, and won't listen. Focusing on your goal in a specific situation often prevents you from achieving it.

Focusing on your goal can also be discouraging. The further off the goal, the harder it seems. Many joggers, before they even run a hundred yards, think about how far they still have to go. "Ugh! Three more miles!" This thought makes their body feel heavy and sluggish. The three miles seem more like three hundred.

The path leading to a long-range goal can *appear* laden with obstacles. William T., an insurance salesman, told me "When I find out that my proposal has to go through many channels before being approved, I get discouraged. The sale seems too far off. Too much can go wrong and probably will. It seems a waste of my time to follow through."

Putting all your attention on something you want to accomplish in the future hinders your performance because it distracts your attention from the present.

# THE ROLE OF GOALS AND DREAMS

Because other people, the economy, competition, politics, or any number of other external factors influences them, goals are out of your control. This doesn't mean you shouldn't have a goal. Goals and dreams are important for providing direction, motivation and inspiration. Without them you can wander and waver like a feather in the wind.

Once you set your goals, however, it's critical to focus all your attention on what you *can do now* to achieve them. Fritz Perls M.D., the father of Gestalt therapy, put it very succinctly. "The Past is gone, the Future not yet. All there is is the Now."

# 18

# CAN-DO THINKING— CONTROLLING THE UNCONTROLLABLE

## CONTROLLED STRESS: A POSITIVE FORCE

Any discussion of the characteristics of performance would be incomplete without mentioning stress in more detail. There is high stress in all three performance zones, but stress isn't always an enemy. Many recent studies have found that stress is important and productive. Stress is like energy and can be very positive if controlled and directed. Out of control, however, it inhibits performance, health, and quality of life.

Lack of control is the reason stress is negative in both the Panic Zone and the Drone Zone. Running around frantically trying to do too much in too little time, the Panic Zoner feels out of control. The Drone Zoner, on the other hand, might have control of his job, but despite his competence, he feels stuck. Afraid to challenge himself further, he feels depressed and in a quandary about what to do.

"According to the latest research," writes award-winning health reporter Susan Seliger, "bad stress is triggered by the feeling that one's decisions are useless, that events are overwhelming and beyond personal control. Positive stress," says Seliger, "comes from rising to challenges, feeling confidence and a sense of control over one's destiny. The ability to control stress is within each person's power. A person who feels in control of his life can channel the stressful energy and make himself healthier and more productive."[1]

"Research shows that people who live life with fervor and purpose have developed ways to cope with stressors," writes cardiologist John M. Kennedy, a board member of the American Heart Association and the author of 'The 15 Minute Heart Cure' "Even in the most maddening, frustrating, and difficult circumstances," continues Kennedy, "you can choose not to become a victim and spiral out of control."[2]

## LISTEN, STOP, LOOK, AND CHOOSE

The first two steps to overcoming the fear and anxiety that causes most stress are discussed in the Conquering Fear chapter (8). Briefly, they begin, as with any illness, by recognizing the symptoms—the self-talk and body signals that indicate stress, such as dry mouth, shortness of breath, heart racing, pain in the neck, and procrastination,.

The second step, which is the first step to gaining control, is to **Stop** and mentally step back from your stress-filled thoughts and take at least three deep breaths. Feel the air slowly fill your lungs, then press with the stomach to exhale the breath. A good exercise is to count slowly to 4 on the inhale, and 6 on the exhale. Rather than being controlled by your anxiety, this step will calm you down so you an see and act more appropriate to the situation.

The next step, as described in detail in chapter 8, is to **Look,** so you can perceive the situation for what it really is, as opposed to how your stress-driven mind makes it seem.

Once you gain a semblance of control and perceive the situation more clearly, it is time to act by refocusing your attention-- to **Choose,** the Can-Do thinking that will put you back in control, enabling you to respond at your best in the situation.

## CAN-DOS

Can-dos increase control of the uncontrollable. When you are planning for anything, from a board meeting to meeting a deadline, there are always elements you can control and those you can't. But you don't have to be a victim of factors out of your control. Identifying these factors is the first step to increasing your control. For every factor not in your control, there will be something you **can do**.

The remainder of this chapter teaches you how to recognize elements and situations that are essentially out of your control and to develop Can-**Do** strategies for dealing with them.

# AFTER FEAR—A CAN-DO

After Alan B., the contractor in a previous chapter, used a reality check to overcome his Drone Zone fear of expanding his business, he made a list of Can-Dos for the expansion. He listed current projects he could bid on, additional equipment he would need, personnel and services needed; made out a budget; and saw a banker to determine whether expansion loans were available.

When your anxiety is running your thinking, your concentration is on what might happen if or when, in the future. When Alan thought about the possible consequences of expanding his business, he became immobilized, too scared even to begin planning. Focusing and acting on Can-Dos-what he could do rather than worry about what he couldn't-shifted his attention from the future, which was out of his control, to the present, and what he could control. This shift moved him out of his Drone Zone immobility.

A Can-Do is empowering. It starts the ball rolling in the right direction and builds momentum, one Can-Do leading to another. This positive action increases confidence and your sense of control. There are four simple characteristics—four C's—of a Can-Do that will ensure an effective response in the most pressured situations:

**Clear-cut.** Can-Dos should translate easily into specific action. Beware of too vague and general commands, such as the ones I gave myself to relax and concentrate in the racquetball game or when I told myself to "slow down" during a talk. I've had many people in programs say they are going to start exercising or giving positive feedback to their employees. " Too general" I tell them. 'When are you going to start, what are you going to do' I always challenge them.

**Constructive**. A Can-Do obviously should be an action that will enable you to improve your performance and continue moving toward your goal. One of my Can-Do's was to make eye contact with three people when I gave a talk which helped me to slow down, improve my contact with the audience and communicate better.

**Current**. A Can-Do is an action that can be started immediately. It is the logical next step based on your experience, ability level and the situation. Although it might relate to a future goal, it is something you **can do now**. Getting on my toes and moving in the racquetball game was a Can-Do that immediately improved my performance. Making eye contact with three people was something I put into action right away.

In your **Control**. A Can-Do is an action over which you have direct control.

## ANTICIPATION VERSUS WORRY

Although you can't control the future, anticipating it is something you **can do** now. There is a big difference between anticipating the future and worrying about it. The worrier, a Panic or Drone Zoner, imagines all the nightmarish possibilities that might occur and feels out of control. Firmly planted in a vicious cycle, the worrier is either too panicked or too paralyzed to act effectively and, therefore, continues to worry.

There are several Can-Dos to anticipate the future and stop worrying. You can speculate, role-play, and preview in the present to develop a repertoire of Can-Do strategies for responding to anything that might occur.

**Speculating** is thinking about any eventualities that might happen and developing responses for them. Most top executives use this strategy for preparing for pressure presentations.

Two of the presidents that were unflappable and incredibly effective in their press conferences were John F. Kennedy and Lyndon Johnson. "Before every presidential news conference, President Kennedy and a half dozen of us would sit down and go over every possible question that he might be asked. When he went to a news conference, he had been briefed to the gills. So, he almost never got a surprise question," reported Dean Rusk, Kennedy's Secretary of State.[3]

**Role-Playing** is "walking a mile in the other person's moccasins" and imagining how it feels. "Lyndon Johnson had a genius for working with a problem from the point of view of the other fellow," according to Dean Rusk. "Putting himself in the other fellow's shoes gave him a considerable understanding of the nature of the problem," Rusk says. "This was one of the attributes that made Johnson a fantastic persuader."[4]

One chief executive officer told us that, before a stockholders' meeting, he goes down to the auditorium and sits in several different seats. "I imagine myself as the person who will be sitting there and see what I would be feeling, thinking, and wanting if I were them. What questions would I have? What would be my concerns? I then figure out how best to respond. I prepare for all important meetings by trying to fully understand the concerns of everyone there."

**Previewing** is visualizing yourself in a future situation, picturing all the things that might come up and imagining what you **can do** to respond to them. Fran Tarkenton, who passed for more yardage than any other quarterback in NFL history did, used previewing to prepare for his upcoming games. "On this week, for example, I would think of Pittsburgh [the opponent] and nothing else. I would see that Steeler defense in my dreams, every one of them, knowing their names, bodies, moves. I must be able to tell who is chasing me by the sound of the footsteps and which way to turn to evade him, for every man has his weakness. I would see those linebackers eyeing me as they backtrack into pass coverage, and know their relative speed and effectiveness. By Friday, I'm running whole blocks of plays in my head . . . I'm trying to visualize every game situation, every defense they're going to throw at me. I tell myself, 'What will I do on their five-yard line, and it's third and goal to go, and our passing game hasn't gone too well, and their line looks like a wall, and we're six points behind?'"[5] Whatever happened in a game was, to Tarkenton, no surprise. He had already pictured a response for almost every possibility.

# WHAT YOU *CAN DO* ABOUT
# THE UNEXPECTED

Inevitably, something that you hadn't planned for occurs. About four years ago, I was caught in traffic on a Los Angeles freeways, which at that moment, resembled a giant parking lot. Nothing was moving. I was on my way to an important meeting, and I knew this jam would make me late—if I got there at all. I was looking to jump lanes, take an emergency exit, or even go up on the grass. But there was no way out.

Then, in a moment of clarity, I took a deep breath and asked myself, "What **can I do** to get this traffic moving or get out of this jam? Nothing", I told myself. "It's out of my control." And with that realization, came an incredible sigh of relief. My whole body relaxed. It was as if a great weight had been lifted from my shoulders. "OK," I said to myself, "what **can I do** now?"

Calming down, I realized that I should text my partner to say I would be late. Then, I chose to rehearse my presentation and to speculate about the people who would be at the meeting and each of their goals and agendas.

After I felt I'd done enough, I turned on some music and did some people watching. When I arrived, I was relaxed and in a positive mood as opposed to the agitation I would have felt if I had just sat in the car pounding the steering wheel.

Even when the unexpected occurs and appears out of your control, you **can** always **do** something that will keep you out of your Panic Zone.

# WHAT YOU *CAN DO* ABOUT ANGER

Focusing on what you can't control causes anger. Whether it is a late report, a frozen computer, or a traffic jam, getting angry is an indication that you feel out of control of the situation. And the more you focus on what you **can't-do**, the angrier and more out of control you feel.

When John T., a manufacturing vice president for a major pharmaceutical company, ranted and raged about the recommendation that his group hadn't finished in time to present to the executive committee, he was focusing on what couldn't be done. Because of this response, he couldn't think clearly enough to determine what could. He could have assessed how late the report would be. He could have called the people coming to the meeting, explained the situation, and perhaps rescheduled it. He might have even developed an alternative plan for summarizing and presenting the material he already had.

The key to breaking the hold of anger is to switch your thoughts from what you can't control to what you **can**. Instead of expending your energy raging about the frozen computer or a late project, you can use the **can-do** to stay in control and direct your energy constructively, instead of blowing it off in a cloud of steam.

## THE SILENT *CAN-DO*

The first time Tim Gallwey and I were conducting an Inner Skiing program together, a ski instructor who obviously had an axe to grind asked Tim a question. Tim stood there thinking for what must have been at least two minutes. I was worried and wanted jump in with a response, but he waved me away. Finally, he came up with a perfect answer. When I asked him later about the pause, he said, "It was a good question and I didn't know the answer. I needed time to think about it."

When asked a difficult question we often think we should have an immediate answer. We fear looking foolish or unprepared if we stop to think. This causes us to respond too quickly and often with a reply not well thought out.

There are many moments when the next step to take or response to make is not immediately clear. The most effective **can-do** at that point is to **stop** and **think.** One can-do that gives you time to think is to credit your questioner by saying; " That's a good question, let me think about it for a minute."

"There's a difference between a speech and a spiel," former Coca-Cola president Don Keough told me. "A lot of speakers are afraid to think while they're speaking. I think it's an enormous tribute to an audience to let them know that you are not only talking to them, but that you're thinking right in front of them. When I sense that a speaker is thinking out loud with me, I feel that he's willing to be vulnerable, willing to let the thoughts that are flowing into his head right at the moment be out there for me to evaluate. I think he's being respectful to me."[6]

# CONTROL CHECK AND *CAN-DO* PLAN

I realize that this Can-Do strategy sounds very simple and obvious. It is. But under pressure, we often forget what we know and overlook the obvious. The first step to remember when under pressure is to **stop**; take a few deep breaths, and assess the situation, this time, by doing a control check and Can-Do plan:

1. List all the factors in the situation that will Influence the outcome. Include everything from the weather and the economy to your client's mood.
2. Review the list, and mark a "C" next to each factor in your control and an "NC" next to each factor not in your control.
3. For each "C," list the Can-Dos.
4. For each "NC," list the Can-Dos that will increase your control in that situation.
5. Prioritizing the Can-Dos from both your "C" and "NC" lists then becomes the basis for an effective action plan.

## *CAN-DO*: CONCENTRATED ACTION

The more focused you are on what you Can-Do Now, the more your concentration intensifies, until you enter into what golfer Tony Jacklin calls "a cocoon of concentration," where nothing distracts you.[7]

One of the greatest tennis players ever, Billie Jean King used to block everything from her focus except one Can-Do.

"I concentrate only on the ball in relationship to the face of my racket, which is a full-time job, since no two balls ever come over the net the same way."[8]

The intense concentration that comes from focusing on what you **can do** will enable you to perform at your peak in the most high-pressure situations.

# 19

# CONDITIONING: GETTING IN SHAPE FOR THE PEAK ZONE

## THE BODY-MIND CONNECTION

The health benefits that accrue from physical conditioning are well known. Less well known is the effect that physical conditioning has on attitude and mental performance. "Body, Mind, and Soul are inextricably woven together," says cardiologist Paul Dudley White, "and whatever helps or hurts one of these three . . . helps or hurts the other two."[1]

Most peak performers we interviewed stressed the importance of being in good physical condition. (Obviously, sports stars know this.) "My physical conditioning is critical to my work. It bothers me mentally if I'm not physically fit," Dick Munroe, the former chairman of Time Inc, told me.

Physician Linda Weinreb, a nationally known authority on the health needs of homeless populations, who maintains a clinical practice, and heads up research for a large medical school says, "When I don't exercise, I'm lethargic and disengaged. I get irritable much more easily and tire more quickly. When I exercise regularly, I'm more vital and positive. I have a feeling of fullness. I'm more present for my patients, and my work is much better."

Your physical condition plays an important part in determining the performance zone in which you will play. A body that is tight and overstressed will break down more easily, need continual attention and limit your effectiveness and productivity. A poorly conditioned body is detrimental to your attitude and enthusiasm, causes mental as well as physical fatigue, and hinders your ability to concentrate and think clearly for long periods of time.

Good physical conditioning increases the likelihood of performing at your best and getting into your Peak Zone. Just as mental attitude affects physical performance, physical conditioning affects mental attitude. Getting to the top demands strength, endurance, and energy whether it is the top of a mountain or the top of your profession. Being in good physical condition helps you to feel better and think clearer; to experience more vitality, energy, and aliveness; and to have more energy, endurance, and strength so that you can perform at your peak more often.

# FOUR COMPONENTS OF FITNESS

Four basic components of a physical conditioning program will get you in shape for playing in your Peak Zone:

1. Aerobic training
2. Flexibility
3. Strength building
4. R & R—relaxation and revitalization

Much has been written about fitness, so I will just outline the basics.

# TYPE C CONDITIONING: 1. AEROBICS

If you were to limit yourself to only one conditioning activity, aerobics would probably[2] be the one to choose. "Aerobics," writes Dr. Kenneth Cooper, author of the ground breaking book, *Aerobics*, "increases the maximum amount of oxygen that the body can process within a given time, called your aerobic capacity. Aerobic training strengthens your heart and lungs and develops a good vascular system."[3] Aerobic exercise enhances attitude and professional performance in many ways.

1. **Increased Energy**. "Now that I exercise regularly, I have more energy to handle the ups and downs of my job and my life and to find solutions to problems that I previously would have been too tired to even think about." Myrtle Harris, former infant and children's wear buyer for a

major national chain, who is now the president of a senior citizens' residential community, told us.

2. **Mental Alertness** "Being in good shape gives me more energy, so I can work faster and longer. I feel more alert, mentally sharp. My thinking is clearer," says Larry Gershman, former president of MGM/United Artists Television Group. "My brain is much sharper after a run, and I can deal with a lot more stress," Peter Thigpen, a past CEO of Levi Strauss Jeans division told me.

3. **Self-confidence**. People in good physical condition tend to have a more positive self-image. The results of a study at Purdue University showed that self-confidence and self-assurance increase as physical conditioning improves. Participants in the study also became more outgoing, more involved with others, and more emotionally stable.

4. **Creativity and Imagination**. "Methinks that the moment my legs begin to move, my thoughts begin to flow," said Thoreau. The Purdue study also confirmed Thoreau's insight that physical conditioning spurs the imagination. It's common knowledge that people often get creative breakthroughs and insights while on a run or a long walk.

5. **Stress Reduction**. Dr. Cooper writes that exercise increases your ability both "to deal with specific stressful situations that occur during the course of each ordinary day  and relieves you of stress at the end of an especially pressure-filled day so that you're more relaxed and energized and ready to work or play, even into the evening hours."[4]

6. **Improved Appearance**. You look more vital, vibrant, and alive. You have more color in your complexion, more muscle tone, and less fat.

7. **Feeling of Well-Being.** Physical exercise helps you to feel better mentally, physically, and spiritually. Many psychologists now prescribe running to combat depression. An added benefit is that exercise generates an abundance of endorphins, which are associated with states of well-being and euphoria.

The physiological benefits of aerobic exercise are well known and equally positive:

- Lower blood pressure.
- Lower resting heart rate—the heart, because it is stronger, does not have to work as hard to transport blood to the rest of the body.
- Increased cardiac output—the heart is better able to distribute blood where needed under stress.
- Increased number of red blood cells—more oxygen can be carried per volume unit of blood.
- Increased elasticity of arteries.
- Lower triglyceride level.
- Decreased blood cholesterol—high-density cholesterol, which is more protective of blood vessels, is proportionately increased.
- Adrenaline secretions in response to emotional stress are lowered.
- Lactic acid is more efficiently eliminated from the muscles, decreasing fatigue and tension.

- Additional routes of blood supply are built up in the heart.

### How Much and How Hard

Although running receives the most publicity, it is hardly the only type of aerobic exercise. Any vigorous activity done for an extended period fits into this category. Walking, swimming, biking, aerobic dance, jumping rope, cross-country skiing, roller-skating, rowing, and square dancing, among other things, can all be done aerobically.

You should do aerobic exercise so that the heart is working in what is called the *target zone.* This level is vigorous enough to strengthen, but not overtax the heart and vascular system. To calculate your target zone subtract your age from 220 (the approximate maximum stroke rate of the heart). Your target zone is between 70 and 85 percent of that number.

For example, if you were 40 years old, it would be

$$220 - 40 = 180$$
$$85\% \text{ of } 180 = 153$$
$$70\% \text{ of } 180 = 126$$

Your target zone would then be between 153 and 126 beats per minute. You should exercise at this rate a minimum of three times per week for 20 minutes per session.

## Starting Out

Many people, after hearing that they have to exercise vigorously for at least 20 minutes a day, three times a week, are overwhelmed. They haven't exercised in years and feel they would be lucky to make it around the block. They're right! Exercising vigorously for 20 minutes a day, three times a week is too much at first. So, do what you **can do** now. Begin slowly. You will probably get into your target zone quite easily at first. Some people who have not exercised for years will get into their target zone by just going out for a brisk walk. So, don't overdo it. Your maximum benefit will come from staying in your target zone. Keep it fun. Make exercise an enjoyable experience, one that you want to do again.

If you are beginning an aerobic training program and are over the age of 35 or physically out of shape, it is wise to get a complete checkup, including a treadmill test.

## Fatigue—Mental or Physical

Often, after a busy day at work, as I am getting ready to go for a run, my self-talk starts out first: "I'm too tired to run today; I think I'll take the day off." Sometimes it's true, my body does need a rest, and it's a good idea to take the day off. Most often, though, it's my mind, that I have been exercising all day, which is tired. The only thing I have done with my body, besides sit, is to go out for lunch.

When I hear that familiar self-talk, I do a reality check to see if I am experiencing physical or mental fatigue. I'll stand up and move around, even jog in place a little, to see how my body feels. With a little practice, you'll be able to discriminate between mental and physical fatigue.

### Heavy Blankets

In response to a question about the most difficult part of his strenuous early-morning workouts, John Akii-Bua, an Olympic gold medalist in the grueling 400-meter hurdles replied, "the blankets." He explained that the blankets in his bed were so warm and comfortable that he had great difficulty lifting them to get out of bed.

If, when the alarm rings, you feel listless and your blankets feel too heavy, remind yourself why you want to exercise in the first place. Take a few minutes to visualize how wide-awake, vital, and full of energy you will feel after you exercise. If you have a specific goal you are shooting for—weighing ten pounds less, looking more attractive, being more energetic at work—visualize yourself accomplishing it.

Michelle K. disliked exercise but loved the energy and power she felt after her 20 minute morning workout. "I'd lie in bed and think about how I'd feel about myself and my ability to handle the day if I had exercised and if I hadn't. That always got me up. A day that I've begun by exercising is a day in which I feel stronger and more energetic. I figure if I can get someone as recalcitrant as me out of a warm bed to exercise, I can do anything!"

## Beating Boredom

One of the more common complaints about aerobic exercise

is that it is boring. Boredom occurs when the mind is out of control and concentrating on what is not happening, rather than what is, and where you'd like to be, rather than where you are.

To combat boredom and increase enjoyment most people exercise using headphones. I listen to some upbeat music that gives me more energy. I have also used tapes to learn Spanish while running and get a lot of reading done while using the exercycle or treadmill in the gym. Acupuncturist Julie Freiberg mentally reviewed the acupuncture points in the body to prepare for her licensing test (she passed). Many people use aerobic time to plan, problem solve, or review their day. A psychologist friend reviews her cases, as she rides her bike. A director of training for a large corporation prepares his programs while running. Other people use their aerobics as an opportunity to get away from people and pressure and to unwind. They dream and fantasize, letting their minds take a breather while their bodies are working.

You can combine fantasy and reality by imagining yourself accomplishing goals you usually only dream about. Allow your imagination to run wild. Let yourself daydream. Besides being fun and energizing, these fantasies can help you learn more about yourself and your desires.

## *Back-Burnering*

A creative process often takes place during exercise. The conscious mind might not be focusing on work during your exercise, but the unconscious is. It's as if there are two burners in the mind. The front burner coincides with the conscious mind, and the back burner, the unconscious. The mind doesn't just drop a problem or a project on which it has been working. It switches it from the front to the back burner.

Therefore, while you are exercising, your unconscious mind is still making connections, searching for answers, developing new perspectives. Back-burner incubation is a critical part of the creative process which is the reason so many people solve problems and get new insights while on a run, a walk, a ride, or swimming laps..

I always bring a recorder with me on my runs or bike rides because I know that, sometime during the time, I will get a new idea or insight into my work. Thomas Hoving, the a past director of New York City's Metropolitan Museum of Art and publisher of *Connoisseur* magazine, said that his most creative ideas came while on his daily bike ride.

## TYPE C CONDITIONING: 2. FLEXIBILITY

My introduction to stretching, which has had a very dramatic effect upon my life, was fortuitous. In my mid-30s, after being extremely athletic for most of my life, I began having lower back pains. After several excruciating episodes, I decided to see an orthopedist. He recommended an operation if I wanted to continue leading a physically active life.

A week and a half before the operation was scheduled, I invited Chuck Nichols, an old friend and former ski instructor to spend the weekend at our house in the country. Early Saturday morning, I found Chuck doing yoga. Their purpose of these poses, he said, was to increase the flexibility of the spine.

He offered to teach me some of the postures. I was skeptical, but the pain in my back was nagging, so I decided I had nothing to lose. He taught me some basic assanas, which we practiced for about a half-hour. I was very relaxed when we finished, and yet, I was full of energy. I practiced the postures several more times that weekend, and my back felt better than it had in a long time. For the next week, I did yoga for 20 minutes both before work and in the evening when I got home. My back felt so good, I canceled the operation.

I have been practicing yoga as well as other forms of stretching every morning since then. My chronic lower back pain is gone. My back is often stiff in the morning, but after 10 to 15 minutes of stretching, it is loose and flexible, and I feel more energized.

Tension saps energy and enthusiasm. Stretching relaxes tense muscles and helps your body remain limber and resilient. It increases energy and range of movement and improves your general feeling of well-being.

Many people use stretching exercises during the day to relieve tension and loosen tight muscles. "I often do a little stretching in the office". Alyce C., the vice president of sales for an equipment-leasing corporation, told us; "A few minutes of stretching, and I feel fresh, more energetic and alert, and my body feels loose and relaxed."

### Loosening Up

You can loosen up when feeling tense anytime and any-where—in your office, commuting, in a meeting—by increasing your tension! Let me explain. It's a natural tendency, when you feel tight, to try to stretch the tense area. But stretching pulls against the tension. Like a tightly coiled spring, a tight muscle will often just spring back to its original tense position after you stop stretching it. And if you pull too hard, if you strain rather than stretch, it will spring back even harder, and you'll have a pulled muscle.

One very effective way to relax a tight muscle is to go with the tension—exaggerate it! If your tension feels like a 5, on a scale of 1-10, tighten it to an 8. Then, **slowly** let go, as you exhale. The voluntary tension you have added to the tight area helps to release the involuntary tension. Then, when you let go, the entire area will begin to relax. From that relaxed position, you can stretch by moving slowly and easily. Remember, it's stretch, not strain. Doing this exercise five times starts the muscle moving, which helps to break the tension and increases its flexibility.

There are many good books on stretching. You can, as I often did when I was learning, take a yoga or stretching class. My wife Marilyn teaches Tri Yoga and, in addition to doing my own stretching every day, I go to her class at least once a week.

Most people know that it's important to stretch before doing aerobic exercises. It's just as important to stretch *after exercising.* Your muscles are then hot from the workout and will stretch more easily at these times.

# TYPE C CONDITIONING: 3. STRENGTH BUILDING

"Just throwing around those weights made me feel stronger and more powerful," Joan G., a vice president of a bank, told us. "This was important because I had always seen myself as weak. Lifting weights changed the image I had of myself. It actually helped me feel more comfortable and confident competing on the job. I feel I can hold my own with anyone now."

Building physical strength helps you to feel stronger mentally. Harold W., a marketing executive who keeps 5- and 10-pound dumbbells in his office, told me that before he started exercising with weights, he felt like the 98-pound weakling in the Charles Atlas ads. "But now, I feel stronger, not just physically, but mentally. Somehow," he said, "the physical strength translated to my psyche. I have more confidence now and feel personally more powerful. I have the courage, I didn't have before, to take the risks I need to."

Strong muscles do more than make you feel powerful. They provide support for the skeleton, resulting in less strain on your bones and ligaments. Building abdominal muscles, for instance, gives you more tone, helps you to look better, and reduces back strain. People's muscles atrophy as they age, so it's important for seniors to prevent muscles from weakening. Remember, if you don't use it, you'll lose it.

There are many ways of building strength at home or in the office by doing push-ups, sit-ups, crunches, and other calisthenics or lifting weights. You can buy a home gym or exerciser. There are also health clubs that will give you an individualized strength-building program for your entire body. If you don't stand around too long between exercise stations at the gym, these programs have an aerobic benefit as well as building strength and muscle tone.

## TYPE C CONDITIONING: 4. R & R (RELAXATION AND REVITALIZATION)

Typical Panic Zoners who work 70- or 80-hour weeks often brag, "My work is my life. I have no hobbies; my job is my only interest." They are working against themselves. "I'm dead against workaholics," says Dick Munroe. "Working like that causes you to lose enthusiasm and vitality and inhibits creativity."

All high-performance systems need a rest cycle. Both mental and physical muscles need rest to revitalize. Without it, they fatigue, lose power and efficiency, and eventually burn out. Therefore, an essential part of a conditioning program is what we call R & R—relaxation and revitalization.

Jim Loehr, the author of *Mental Toughness,* a former sports psychologist who now operates a wellness center writes, "To create optimal performance, you have to address the management of energy at every level." Loehr says, "What we've found is very simple. The more ways that people are encouraged to oscillate—to move between stress (and relaxation)—anything that prompts the expenditure of energy and recovery, the happier they are, the better they perform, and the higher their productivity level."[5]

In the Peak Performance workshops I conduct, we give participants three 10-minute "time-out" cards and tell people that they have to use them each day. R & R periods can vary in time and intensity from a long vacation to a five-minute break in the middle of a pressure-filled day. They can be physically active or meditationally tranquil. The key aspect of R & R is to take a mental and physical break from what you are doing.

## Destressing

Stress is cumulative. It keeps building with each pressure event of the day. Let's say you start out the day at a base stress level of 3 (on a scale of 1–10). An angry phone call can jolt your stress up to a 6. After you handle the situation, your stress will decrease, but not to the level where it was before the phone call. It might now be a 4. A few more tense situations, and your base stress level is a 6.

If you don't reduce your stress, it will continue to build. By the time you leave the office, your stress could be staggeringly high causing you to be irritable and preoccupied. You might lose your temper and become extremely agitated over the least little thing. Or you might try to drown out the day and everything else with alcohol. If this continues, your base stress level the next day will be even higher.

An R & R break at the end of the day will decrease your stress. But when you have been engrossed in a problem or project, it's difficult to simply stop thinking about it and relax. Diverting your attention is much more effective.

Many people find exercise to be a form of R & R. Physical

exercise of any kind is a great way to bring closure to your workday. It will help to sweat out accumulated tension, get your blood moving and oxygenate your system, which will increase your energy level and revitalize you.

Former US Senator William Proxmire who used to walk at the end of the day said; "I can start off tired and weary after a long day in the Senate, with all kinds of frustration, feeling too tired to sleep and far too tired to walk . . . After the first difficult quarter- or half-mile, not only does my frustration ease . . . I feel more rested and fully alert."[6]

But an R & R break doesn't have to be physically vigorous. The president of a major publishing house makes chairs. A well-known network-television news reporter plays the piano for half an hour at the end of the day to relax and unwind. A vice president of a large brokerage firm loves to tinker with the engine of her car when she gets home from work. "It's like therapy," she told us. "I get so involved that I forget the troubles of the day. There's also a great feeling when I fix something."

It doesn't matter what you do to relieve your stress at the end of the day. The key to R & R is involvement in something satisfying and engrossing that takes your mind off the job.

## Working Late

Because it decreases stress and increases energy, an end-of-the-day R & R break will help you become more productive if you do have to work late. When I worked in advertising, I played in a softball league between 6 p.m. and 8 p.m. After playing, I would often return to the office. I found that after a ball game, I had much more energy and was more creative and productive. On the other hand, when I hadn't taken an R & R break and had either skipped dinner or had a quick bite at my desk, I tired much earlier. My enthusiasm and energy were lower, and the quality of my work wasn't nearly as good.

Many people are very productive late at night. A senior partner in a Wall Street law firm said that she does her most creative work between 10 p.m. and midnight. "It's quiet in the house. The phone isn't ringing, and no one bothers me, so I can concentrate without distractions and get a lot done. But," she told us, "if I didn't take a break and relax after work, I'd be too exhausted to do anything. This way, I get two more productive hours and have still spent some quality time with my family."

## Shifting Gears: Taking a Time-Out

A well-known syndicated columnist told me that when he is stuck writing, he will stop and shift his attention. "I may do a menial task, some trashy reading, which doesn't require a lot of heavy thinking, play some tennis, or even go to a movie. It's too bad there are no showers at work. I get some of my best ideas there.

"I don't have any hard and fixed rules about what I should do at these times," he continued. "I just have to take my mind off the article I'm writing. I've done as much as I can, my mind needs a rest. Invariably, either during or right after my break,

I will get a flash—I don't know how else to describe it—that gives me some new insight or perspective."

When pressure becomes overwhelming, an athlete, or a team, takes a time-out to calm down and assess the situation. Pausing to revitalize yourself in the middle of a pressure-filled day will enable you to work for longer periods with less fatigue and loss of concentration. To realize the fullest benefits of these R & R breaks, it's important to "disconnect" mentally, as well as physically, from the pressure.

"I've been a golf nut ever since I can remember, so when my mind starts to race in all directions, I take out my putter and a few balls and practice putting for a couple of minutes," Harvey K., a broadcasting executive, told me. "It takes all of my attention to get that ball into the cup. This little break relaxes me, and I'm better able to concentrate when I get back to work."

In the middle of the day, when he feels tired, psychologist and author Dr. David Brandt will often sit back in his chair, put on earphones, closes his eyes and listen to some electronic music. It so captivates him, he says, that for those moments, he forgets the day. "The music relaxes me and gives me a lift so that after five minutes or so, I feel refreshed, energized, and ready to go again. The earphones are great because they drown out everything else."

When he was overwhelmed with phone calls, copy changes, and shortened deadlines, graphic designer Peter Bailey would stop and do a five-minute routine he learned while studying t'ai chi. At the end of it, he said, "I feel like a new person, calmer and with a lot more energy."

## Taking a Five-Minute Vacation

Joanna S., a marketing executive, uses visualization to help her relax in the middle of a hectic day. She closes her office door, stops her calls, sits back in her chair, and takes a five-minute trip to her favorite beach in Hawaii. "I feel as if I am really there," she told us. "In my mind, I see the colors of the ocean, the trees, the sand, the sky. I put as much detail as I can into the scene, which makes it seem more real. Sometimes I actually hear the ocean, feel the warm sand and the air on my face, and even smell the sea. After a few minutes 'at the beach', I feel renewed and full of energy. I feel like I can handle anything that comes up."

## Beating the Blahs: Taking an Oxygen Break

The "blahs"—we all know what they are. Just before lunch, you run out of steam. Around four o'clock, you start feeling drowsy and unfocused. One cause of the "blahs" is a lack of oxygen. The combination of minimum physical activity and maximum stress results in shallow breathing, which reduces oxygen. We feel sluggish, and concentration is difficult.

Often we'll take a coffee break to try and combat this feeling and get a needed energy boost. But coffee and/or sugar only work for a brief period. After an hour or so, the bodies' chemical reactions brought about by sugar or caffeine result in a sharp drop in energy.

You can get a needed energy boost without the detrimental or addictive effects of caffeine and sugar by oxygenating your system. Doing moderate exercise, something that gets you breathing a little more heavily, but not sweating, will give you a burst of energy. I do some push-ups, half sit-ups or lift some light weights, when I feel sluggish at work. You can take a quick walk around the block. We know an executive who will walk up a few flights of stairs, which he says, "gets my heart pumping and gives me some energy as well as some time out of my office and away from the phone and people."

The top half of a jumping jack is especially effective. Moving your arms up and down rapidly for two or three minutes increases your heart rate, which oxygenates your system and invigorates you. One executive we interviewed had a rowing machine in his office; another, a stationary bike. When they felt logy, they would take a little energy break.

When I taught, I always preferred a schedule of morning classes. The students were more mentally alert then, and so was I. In the afternoon, they were lethargic, fuzzy in their thinking, and just generally less present. One semester, I had to schedule two afternoon classes but remedied the situation by starting each class with five minutes of vigorous exercise. The change was amazing! Everyone was much more awake and alert. Our thinking was clearer and crisper, and we were all more enthusiastic.

## Tension/Release

An effective means of easing tension is the loosening-up method we discussed earlier. Briefly, further tighten an already tense muscle, and then slowly release it. Tensing and releasing a tight muscle starts it moving, which breaks the tension, and automatically begins to relax it. Coordinate these movements with your breath. Tighten the tense muscle on an inhale. Hold it in that position as you hold your breath. Then, slowly release the muscle in time with an exhale.

To relax completely from head to toe, work your way up your body, tensing and releasing each muscle group in time with your breathing. Try it now. Begin at the bottom. Tense your feet as you inhale for a count of four—curl your toes, tighten your arch, and tense your entire foot. Hold your feet tense, as you hold your breath for a count of two. Then, slowly relax them as you exhale for a count of six. Gradually work your way up your body, tensing and releasing each major muscle group—calves, thighs, buttocks, stomach, back, arms, shoulders, face—in time with your breath and counting: in for four . . . hold for two . . . out for six . . .

## Relaxation Triggers

The effect of relaxation exercises is cumulative. The more you practice them, the easier it becomes to be calm and composed in pressure situations. If you initially take 10 to 15 minutes to do a deep-breathing or tension/release exercise, the body's sense memory will begin to remember the effects of the exercise. You will soon be able to bring about the same result by tensing and releasing only one muscle group.

Dr. Julie Anthony, a clinical psychologist and former world-ranked tennis player who was on the staff of the Philadelphia Flyers hockey team, taught relaxation exercises to the players in which "the player sits in a relaxed position and progressively tenses and relaxes all the major muscles in his body." Regarding the triggering effect of these exercises, she said, "Practicing this twice a day for 15 minutes, he eventually can take a few breaths, tense and relax a few muscles, and feel his entire body relax. In the game, if the score is close, and he is waiting to go in, he can use this technique to keep himself from getting too tight. Or if he has just been involved in a brawl, he can skate around for a few seconds, use the relaxation technique, and then be able to play effectively."[7]

Bill Kennedy, the national sales manager for a management-training corporation, explained how he uses the triggering effect of these relaxation exercises. "In a tense meeting, I will hold my hands behind my back, or under the desk, and tighten and loosen my fist a few times in time with my breathing. It really helps me to relax and stay calm under pressure."

## Vacations

Getting away from the pressure-filled work environment for a couple of days or weeks is mentally, physically, and spiritually revitalizing. An AT&T executive told us that takes a vacation to ski or play tennis, he does nothing related to business. "A diversion really recharges me."

"After a vacation, I'm excited about getting back to work," Tony Morgan, a former board member of the B.B.C., Olympic silver medalist in sailing, and successful entrepreneur, told us. "I'm enthusiastic and energized. My perceptions are sharper. I see things much clearer than before I left."

It's quite common to see old problems with new eyes after

spending a week hiking, skiing, scuba diving, white-water rafting, or just relaxing on a beach. And as we mentioned, you might even get some new ideas. Clarence Birdseye built a giant company and revolutionized the retail food industry from an insight he gained on a fishing trip. Noticing an Eskimo practice of keeping their fish frozen in ice gave him the idea for frozen food. I guess that trip was worth the price.

## CONDITIONING FOR THE PEAK ZONE

A finely tuned body is an invaluable asset for anything you will do in your life. The physical qualities of strength, flexibility, energy, and endurance that you develop from a conditioning program automatically transfer to the mental, enabling you to think more clearly and be able to concentrate for longer periods. Being in good physical shape increases your self confidence providing the energy and courage to push past previous limits and stay in that Peak Zone for longer periods.

# 20
# FUELING THE FIRE

Leaders and peak performers in all fields often aren't the smartest or most skilled, but they are the ones with fire in the belly. They're passionate about what they do. Passion is a burning commitment that infuses your entire being—Body, Mind, and Spirit—making you feel more vital and alive and enabling you to tap into inner strengths, resources, skills, and energy you didn't know existed.

You can be highly skilled and confident but if you don't have the fire in the belly, you aren't going to succeed. Passion is the key for turning ideas into action, for excelling in anything you do, and for getting the creative juices flowing. It is the essential ingredient for facilitating the implementation of the ideas and strategies discussed in this book. It is the inner fire that enables ordinary people to accomplish extraordinary things.

## PERSEVERANCE

Perseverance is often touted as the key to success. But passion is the precursor for the perseverance needed to succeed.

A friend told me the following story regarding this type of dedication. At a public gathering, someone in the audience told golfing great Gary Player, the most successful international golfer of all time and the only modern golfer to win the prestigious British Open in three different decades, "I'd give anything if I could hit a golf ball like you."

"No, you wouldn't!" responded Player. "Do you know what it takes to hit a golf ball like me?" Player asked. "You've got to get up at 5:00 every morning, go out to the golf course, and hit a thousand balls. Your hands start bleeding, and you walk to the clubhouse and wash the blood off your hands, slap a bandage on it, and go out and hit another thousand golf balls! That's what it takes to hit a golf ball like me."

It takes an incredible amount of perseverance and hard work to reach the top, whether it is in a sport or at work, but without that fire in the belly you won't get through the pain, doubts, and other obstacles necessary to reach your goal. Passion is the fuel that powers perseverance in anything you do. Without that inner fire, perseverance soon fades like a dying ember, along with your goals and dreams.

## MOUNTAINS AND MOLEHILLS

Passion shapes your perception. The more fired up you are, the less difficult a task seems. Mountains seem like molehills. Anything seems possible. Nothing seems too much trouble or too difficult. You see obstacles that would normally throw you as challenges to overcome, when you are passionate about what you are doing.

On the other hand, when the fire is low, everything seems overwhelming. Molehills seem like mountains. The smallest obstacle seems insurmountable. Everything becomes too much trouble, too difficult. When energy and enthusiasm are low, it feels as if you have to push through a wall of resistance to accomplish anything.

## IT'S NOT WORK

When you are excited about what you do, you spend more time practicing, learning, and trying to improve. People who love golf, for instance, spend hours at the driving range; they buy books and magazines, watch tapes, keep up with the latest innovations, share tips, take lessons. Their passion for the game fuels all this extra effort.

The same is true with anything you are excited about. When I worked in advertising, I spent many an evening watching television, but not the programs, the commercials. I was so fired up about my job that I would try to think of approaches that were more creative for the products advertised. It wasn't work; it was fun.

When asked what he was looking for when hiring people, Shantanu Narayen, CEO of Adobe Systems the recognized software innovator which for 25 years has revolutionized how the world engages with ideas and information, said; "For me, the biggest predictors of success are raw intelligence and passion for what you do. I try to look for people who are going to have a tremendous passion for being here, as opposed to this just another job."[1]

# PASSION LEADS TO INNOVATION

When you're passionate about something, you also become more resourceful often discovering and developing innovative new ideas, products, or services.

As a young man, Jack O'Neill loved the water. He surfed, scuba dived, fished, and always managed to work in or around the water. The problem that O'Neill and his friends encountered was that the water in the San Francisco Bay area was cold. The wetsuits the surfers used leaked and were cold, limiting their time in the water. Driven by his desire to spend more time in the ocean, O'Neill began experimenting with materials and designs that would be leakproof and warm. His search resulted in the first warm, leakproof wetsuit. Today, it's rare to go to a beach without seeing O'Neill wetsuits, surfboards, and a load of other water sport products. And when I interviewed Jack, he still loved the water and lived in a boat on the California coast.

# THE PASSION INDEX

At a series of change-management seminars I conducted for Hewlett Packard, managers were instructed to bring in a change project—a new idea for a process, program, system, or strategy they wanted to implement back at work.

The first step in the program was for each manager to rate his or her project on a *passion scale* of 1–10, with 10 being fired up about it and 1, a dying ember. After conducting these seminars with managers from all over the world for five years, we found that  a project at 7 or below on the passion scale, wouldn't get done. Our advice, when the fire was low, was to return to the drawing board and redesign the project so that they would be more excited about it or to rethink it altogether using passion as their guiding element.

How passionate are you about what you are doing? What is your passion index about the project you are working on or your job? If it's below an 8, it's time to go back to the drawing board and rethink or reinvent what you are doing, using passion as your guide.

## LIGHT THE FIRE

Ultimately, passion will enable you to do more than you ever thought possible and be more than you ever thought you could be. When you are passionate about what you are doing, you'll tap into skills and inner resources you didn't know existed. That inner fire is the key to transforming  innate potential into peak performance.

When you are excited about what you are doing, you'll find that nothing is too hard, no peak too high, no dream impossible, and you'll enjoy the climb as much as reaching the summit.

The next chapter outlines techniques for lighting the fire.

# 21
# STOKE FIRES...
# DON'T SOAK THEM

You're off to a meeting, and you're stoked. You've got this great idea for a new service that will differentiate you from the competition and will give you a huge leap forward. It's a real barnburner, and you can't to present it to your boss. Well, hold on to your shirt and maybe go back to your office to get a raincoat because you can expect to get fire hosed.

*Fire hosing* is the most common response to change, innovative new ideas and out-of-the-box thinking. It's the voice of resistance that always tells you why your ideas won't work, can't be done, and aren't in the budget, anyway. As Albert Einstein once said, "The greatest ideas are often met with violent opposition from mediocre minds." Adding to that, the great German philosopher Arthur Schopenhauer said that all truths are either initially ridiculed or violently opposed.[1]

Fire hosing often seems wise because it ties into past experience—"the way we've always done it." Most often, the wise old veteran who has "seen it all" is the most active fire hoser. This old vet's negative response vet seems to inject some control into an uncertain, world. It is the safe response. But attempting to stay in the comfort zone in a world of constant change quickly becomes very uncomfortable and leads to the Drone Zone. Playing it safe is dangerous in a constantly changing, increasingly competitive environment. Playing it safe is playing not to lose, which most often results in losing.

Although fire hoses often sound reasonable, they are destructive for three reasons. First, they kill an idea that might be good but needs a little twist or different spin. *So, fire hosing kills creativity.* Second, when's the next time you'll come up with a new idea after you have been fire hosed? How about never. *Fire hosing kills motivation and participation.* Third, they douse the spark and dampen enthusiasm. *Fire hosing kills the spirit.*

Guess who we fire hose most often? Right, *ourselves.* Before we even write down our idea or give anyone else a chance to respond to it, our self talk showers us with a multitude of reasons why: "it won't work," "can't be done," and "they'll never buy it." *So, fire hosing ourselves kills our own creativity, motivation, and spirit.*

## OLD HABITS DIE HARD

One reason the fire hose is the most common response to something new and out of the box is that we're all creatures of habit. Habits, the old, automatic responses to anything new, put you to sleep mentally and deaden your spirit. They keep you "in the old box" doing things the same way you have always done them, insuring that learning, growth, and creativity won't happen. Old habits in a new environment quickly turn into ruts, and what do most people do when in a rut? They try to get comfortable with their discomfort, like furnishing the rut.

The reason people fire hose new ideas is that they feel strange and uncomfortable. Try this little habit-breaking exercise, and you'll understand what I mean: Cross your arms. Now, cross them with the other arm on top. Notice how it feels. Weird, right? Like you've lost your armpit. Clap your hands. Now, clap them with what was your bottom hand on top. How does that feel? Strange and uncomfortable, right?

The bottom line when trying something new is that it's usually not going to feel comfortable. How could it? You've never done it before. When you face doing something that feels strange, uncomfortable, and uncertain or something familiar and "tried and true," what will you choose? The most common and easiest response is to resist the new and go back to the old. Old habits die hard. But keep in mind the words that one CEO told me—*"the tried and true is dead and needs to be buried."*

## GETTING THE HABIT OF BREAKING OLD HABITS

One of my rules is to make it a habit to break one habit every week. Do something different both at work and at home. Start with something easy. Take a different route home from work. Eat with your opposite hand. Put your pants on starting with your opposite leg. Brush your teeth with your other hand. Go somewhere for lunch you haven't gone before, and eat something you haven't tried. At work, you might try to attack the mountain of paper or e-mails by starting at the bottom. The ideas is to get comfortable with change, with trying new things-- to get in the habit of breaking your habits.

I give more than 75 speeches a year, and none of them is the same. I always try at least one new story, example, or exercise in every presentation I give. I often even shift the focus of the entire talk. Trying something new keeps me fresh and on my creative edge. It prevents me from falling into the Drone Zone and just "phoning it in" with a canned presentation that I am comfortable with. Since I'm not sure the new addition will work, this strategy is also anxiety producing, which helps because, like most people, I concentrate better and have more energy when I am a little scared. An added benefit is that after four or five speeches, I have a completely new program to offer to clients.

## DODGING THE FEAR SPRAY

Fear is one of the major causes of fire hosing. People are scared that the new idea won't work, that they can't learn the new skill, or that they won't be needed if the idea succeeds. The response, therefore, is to hose the idea, so they can be safe and comfortable.

To dodge the fear fire hose, it helps to understand, as has been discussed in the fear chapter, that most fears are exaggerated, and the imagined difficulty and consequences of something not working are usually blown out of proportion. So, when you catch yourself fire hosing one of your own ideas because you're afraid; it won't work, you'll look foolish, or be fired, do a reality check. A strong dose of reality thinking will enable you to see; what is *true* about the situation, your ability to deal with it, and that the consequences aren't as bad as your fear-driven mind makes them seem.

Remember to ask yourself:

1. "What is the worst thing that can happen if this idea doesn't work?"
2. "On a scale of 1–10, what is the likelihood of that (worst thing) happening?"

Just asking the two reality thinking questions is enough in itself to block the hose. Checking your victory log of past successes and reviewing it when starting on something new is also very helpful for increasing confidence and reducing fire hosing.

## WIIFM

Another cause of the fire hose is the "what's in it for me" response. When people don't see any *personal gain* from an innovative new idea, they're usually not going to be motivated to act on it. With no incentive for taking on a new approach that often necessitates additional work, learning or risk, the hose quickly emerges.

Often when a C-level executive outlines a new approach or direction, many employees aren't motivated, in fact, quite the opposite. "So, we get to increase our share of market and bottom line, and become no. 1," one mid-level manager said to me, "What do I get out of all that, except more work with fewer resources?" How hard do you think that guy is going to work to implement the new strategy?

## TOP DOWN HOSES

When people aren't asked for their input on a new ideas that involves them, they feel dumped on and resent it—"How come no one asked for my input?" And they turn on the faucets. Not feeling part of the solution, they often will become part of the problem in implementing it. Personal involvement in a new idea is incredibly motivating. When people or teams are involved in developing a new idea or part of it, they will be much more positive about it and go to the wall to make it happen.

The best way to plug up the fire hose when you are introducing a new idea is to anticipate these types of resistance. Make sure to mention how you are going to prepare the group for change eg a new training program to get them up to speed. Discuss the incentive for changing. Let them know what's in it for them if the idea or new direction is successful, and get them involved in some way or other in some phase of the idea's development. At a major telecom facility where a completely new accounting system was being introduced, management countered the resistance by having each department customize the system for its group.

# DON'T ARGUE

It usually doesn't work to argue with "hosers." Attempting to overcome a fire hoser's resistance with rational reasoning is usually a no win situation. An innovative idea is often un-conventional and counterintuitive, so rational reasons won't work. And if an idea is too rational and practical, someone else has probably done it already.

Paul Hawken, an internationally known environmentalist and founder of Smith & Hawkins Garden Stores, whose books have been published in more than 50 countries and been the basis for a 17-part PBS series, once told me that "If 90% of the people think your new idea is great, you' re too late. On the other hand," Hawken said, "if 90% tell you it's lousy, will never work, you may be on to something."

# NURFING THE HOSE

One way to dodge the spray of the fire hose is to use the rath-er unconventional technique described below, which is both effective and fun.

At a brainstorming session on reinventing the future with the leaders of a large hospital chain, I placed a large red Nerf ball on the table and announced that anyone who fire hosed any idea was fair game to have the ball thrown at them.

After about 15 minutes, one vice president responded to one idea with "That's too expensive and we've already got our budget worked out. What's more, the docs and nurses will never go along with it anyway."

Boom! Someone hit him with the Nerf ball. Everyone laughed—even the hoser. And that was the signal for open fire on all hosing. It was incredible. Every time someone came out with a fire hose, he got Nerfed. One manager even threw the ball at another claiming it was for being firehosed three weeks ago.

The fun was contagious and the change in the group was startling, managers who previously had been quiet, standoffish or openly skeptical got actively involved. And everyone started piggybacking on other people's ideas and coming up with many out-of-the-box suggestions, laughing all the while. At one point, the group's chief operating officer took the ball and threw it in his own face, announcing, "If you would have heard what I was thinking, you would have Nerfed me, too, so I beat you to it!"

An added benefit of this type of exercise is that when people are having fun, they're more  relaxed and less inhibited, so you get increased participation. Furthermore, when you are having fun, you operate out of the same side of your brain that creativity and intuition comes from. So, fun in these instances is a precursor to increased involvement and creativity—*joy pays!*

The result of the meeting was the development of a line of information software for  external health facilities, which was doing  than $85 million in three years. And believe me; it wouldn't have happened without that crazy red Nerf ball.

Almost weekly, I receive Nerf balls or other alternatives such as water pistols, with company logos and notes saying, "We

Performance Under Pressure

use these at all of our meetings." Several months ago, one client mailed me a Super Soaker, one of those big Tommy gun-type water pistols, with a note; "We've got big hosers in our place."

The key to keeping out in front of change and developing innovative new ideas, possibilities, and opportunities is to *stoke fires, not soak them*. Bring along your Nerf ball the next time you're going to a meeting and be ready for some action, fun, and creativity. Keep one handy in your office. I have a water pistol in my desk drawer, and whenever I catch myself fire hosing one of my own ideas, I give myself a little squirt.

## DODGING THE SPRAY

To prepare you to anticipate resistance to change and new ideas, I have listed some of the more typical fire hoses:

"That isn't the way we do things around here."
"This is the way we've always done it."

Doing things the way you always have ensures you won't change and, therefore, probably won't be around much longer. Using yesterday's strategies and practices in today's game will almost guarantee you won't be around tomorrow.

**"Great idea, but!"**
This is code for "I think the idea stinks." Anything that comes after the but is bull.

**"Don't stick your neck out."**
An ostrich, "bury your head in the sand," strategy can't

possibly work in a competitive environment. If you don't stick your neck out, you'll lose your head. The old comfort zone won't be comfortable for long. The only thing comfortable in this type of environment is the excitement resulting from change and innovation.

**"It's just a fad."**

Today's fad is often tomorrow's necessity.

**"It's too..."**

hard, complicated, expensive, quick, slow, showy, takes too long. Anytime you hear the word *too*, it is too late.

**"It'll never work; can't be done."**

And neither could most of the things you are doing right now. Don't forget what was impossible and couldn't be done yesterday will be by tomorrow.

**"They'll never buy it."**

Just as they' d never pay $3.00 for a cup of coffee, pay money for a bottle of water, or air for your tire, buy a car from a woman, elect an African-American president. Should I continue?

**"It is unrealistic or impractical."**

What was realistic yesterday is probably outdated today and will be obsolete tomorrow. And what seems unrealistic today will probably be common practice tomorrow.

**"If it ain't broke, don't fix it."**

If you wait until it's broke before you try to fix it, you'll end up with nothing left to fix and probably be broke.

**"Don't rock the boat."**

Huge waves of change are already rocking the boat and will sink it if you're not prepared to change course.

**"It's not in the budget."**

Of course not. This year's budget was made last year when circumstances were entirely different.

**"Let's wait and see."**

A delay tactic based on the hope that down the road the entire idea will be forgotten. And by the time you wait to see if something works, the opportunity will have flown away on someone else's wings.

The key to remember is to **stoke the fires, not soak them.**

# 22
# DREAMS ARE GOALS WITH WINGS

Several years ago, the Defense Department sent out bids for a new computer system for one of its jet fighters. A relatively minor research investment by the winning bidder would be necessary to develop the new system. But since the contract was for $90 million, everyone at the contractor, who seemed certain to get the job, was excited. Top management's last word regarding the request for the research money was "Go ahead with it…." Then, the fire hose hit—"…as long as it doesn't impact next quarter's numbers." It did. They didn't get the contract.

Is this a true story? Unfortunately, it is, and it illustrates the mindset prevailing in many companies in this country. As a culture, on both the individual and the organizational level, we have developed a fast food mentality—we want instant gratification, instant recognition, and instant profit.

# SHORT-TERM AND SHORTSIGHTED

One thing Victor Kiam hated when he was president and chairman of Benrus Watch Co. was the focus on short-term results and having to answer to the stockholders about them. "We were constantly saying if we do this now, what's it going to do to our earnings in this quarter?"[1]

In the dogged pursuit of short-term goals and the bottom line, we have developed cultural myopia. All our hopes and inspirations relate to making next quarter's numbers. With this foreshortened field of vision, we live and die by the quarter.

"We need to break out of this linear short-term thinking that assumes you set goals at the beginning of a period, manage your company around those goals, then evaluate performance and reward people when, presumably, the goals are achieved," says former Bank of America senior vice president K. Shelly Porges. "It's too constricting. We need to enlarge ourselves and our perspectives and recognize that goals may change during the period in pursuit of vision."[2]

# RIGID GOALS, FRIGID RESULTS

One year Chris Evert's goal was to win Wimbledon and to be ranked first in the world. She did both and experienced that great feeling of accomplishment you get when you achieve a hard-won victory. But, she said it lasted only 25 minutes. Then, it was back to reality and on to the next goal.

Many of us have had a similar experience of living for a

goal and, upon reaching it, feeling let down. You work hard all year to "make the numbers," and at the year's end, you have that bittersweet realization that next year's goals will be upped, and last year's record-breaking performance will be as exciting as yesterday's news. It's like constantly reaching the carrot which is continually being pulled out of reach.," a friend of mine said, "It gets old really fast."

I have a friend who has his own small insurance company. He has seven agents working for him, and each year, they set aside time to establish the goals of the following year. "I gotta tell you," he confided, "each year it gets harder and harder to get them pumped up. We usually make our goals, and everyone makes good money. We celebrate, have a little party, a dinner, everyone gets a bonus, and then it starts all over again."

It's no wonder that, according to research by Dr. Ron Lippitt, "During the course of goal-setting meetings, participants become more and more depressed. This discouragement occurs in part because [the process] reinforces the belief that the future will be no different from the past."[3]

## "GOALS ONLY LIMIT YOU"

In the relentless pursuit of the next quarter's bottom line, we fail to value anything that doesn't have a linear relation to making the numbers. Such tunnel vision blinds us to opportunities for innovation and creativity. It prevents us from seeing other possibilities that might appear because of change, new technologies, or an unpredicted circumstance. As a result, the mad-dash rat race to make the short-term numbers hinders our creativity, our motivation and our spirit. Ultimately, specific short-term goals limit the imagination and inhibit innovation.

Summing up this fixation on short-term goals and objectives, Scott McNeally, founder of Sun Microsystems, said that the motto at the company is "Goals only limit you."

## GOALS ARE SECONDARY

Having goals is not the problem. What gets us into trouble is the importance we attach to them. Goals have their place—second place, following dreams or vision. They serve a purpose. They give us a specific target to shoot at and provide feedback to tell us how we are doing. They are a way of keeping score. But if goals are to be beneficial for enhancing performance, productivity, and motivation, they must be guided by something larger and more encompassing, something that inspires us and infuses us with passion, creativity, and courage.

## OLYMPIC STARTING BLOCKS

Many years ago, I was talking about goal setting to John Naber, the TV broadcaster who had won four gold and one silver medal in swimming at the '76 Olympics. He said he used goal setting extensively during his training. He set very specific goals for each event, including daily, weekly, monthly, and quarterly objectives, some of which involved improving his time by thousandths of a second.

He told me that having specific goals helped him a great deal in measuring his progress. But those goals were just a step toward achieving a larger dream, a means to an end. One thing was much more exciting to him, without which, he felt he wouldn't have accomplished nearly as much. It was the dream of winning the gold medal and being the world champion that kept him going through all the days and years of hard practice.

Not a day went by when Naber didn't see himself on top of the victory stand with a gold medal around his neck and the flag going up. He could hear the National Anthem playing and the crowd cheering. Without that vision, no goal setting in the world would have helped.

Successful people in all occupations echo Naber. The key to sustained peak performance is finding something larger than a goal, something bigger to shoot for. Something that moves you. A dream you can chase. An inspiring vision.

## LBV—LEADERSHIP BY VISION

"My thinking has really been turned on its head," says Donald Povejsil, former vice president of corporate planning for Westinghouse. "Ten years ago, I believed the key [to success] was tightly reasoned analysis of markets and competitors." Yet, at the small and very successful business units Westinghouse created, Povejsil saw people making decisions based on a vision rather than a narrow set of goals.

"I could detect a distinct correlation between this vision and the performance of these 20 or so business units. The good ones had a vision. As for the bad ones, it was hard to tell why they came to work in the morning...Vision is the linchpin of strategic management—there's no other conclusion you can reach after a while."[4]

A poll of *Fortune* 500 CEOs confirmed Povejsil's realization. When asked what will characterize top leadership traits in the decade to come, number one on the list was vision.[5] Organizations need a vision to fire people up, engage the spirit, and provide direction.

Just as an organization, we each need a personal vision or dream to fuel the fire in our heart, provide more meaning to our efforts, and encourage us to confront the challenges lying ahead.

## WE DID THE IMPOSSIBLE

Dreams can empower people as nothing else. A wonderful example is the now well-known story of Eugene Lang, millionaire entrepreneur from the South Bronx. In his late sixties, Lang was asked to talk to students at the junior high school from which he had graduated. The years had taken their toll on the South Bronx, and it little resembled the Central European, immigrant community of his childhood. Now, it was a battlefield of poverty, drugs, and gangs and a breeding ground of despair and hopelessness.

Lang had prepared a speech for the graduating eighth-graders designed to "motivate them" with the conventional wisdom, "If I can do it, you can too." After looking out at an audience that clearly wasn't interested in him, Lang threw away his prepared speech and said one thing, "If you graduate from high school" (typically about 20 percent of the youth of the South Bronx would earn a high school diploma), "I will send you to college."

Four years later, the result was phenomenal. All but two of the 60 kids finished high school, and many had gone on to the best colleges. When the media asked them about their success, they said, "He gave us hope; he gave us a chance to dream; he gave us a golden opportunity." One student, upon meeting Lang later, rightly said, "Mr. Lang, we did the impossible."

When we have a dream and pursue it, nothing is impossible. We tap into power, personal resources, and creativity we never thought we had. We can accomplish what previously had been considered impossible. In the process, we discover that the biggest limit is our mind telling us what our limits are.

## BURGER KING UNIVERSITY

The owner of a Mid-Atlantic Burger King franchise constantly faced the industry dilemmas of language problems, high employee turnover (60 percent per year), and consequent high recruiting and training costs ($40,000 a year). Taking heart from Lang's example and with a generous dash of courage, he found a solution. He offered to pay college tuition for employees staying with him for four years. That's the only thing he changed. "You stay with me; I'll pay tuition for you." Two years into the new "fringe benefit" program, his turnover is down to 9 percent, and his training cost has been reduced by 75 percent.

# DREAMS ARE GOALS WITH WINGS

Like most creative functions, dreams are housed in the right hemisphere of the brain, along with passion, imagination, and emotions including joy. Goals, rational, linear, and measurable, on the other hand, form in the left hemisphere. The dream is an ideal state, the goal a real state. The dream supplies the passion, vigor, vision, and direction; the goal, a specific, short-term target and the strategies for hitting it. The goal is a step toward the dream.

A dream supplies meaning and intrinsic value. It is our deepest expression of what we want, a declaration of a desired future. It involves a sense of possibilities rather than probabilities, of potential rather than limits. Goals set without a dream use literally only half of our brainpower. The passion is missing when we just work with our rational left-brain.

A dream is the wellspring of passion, providing direction and pointing us to lofty heights. It is an expression of optimism, hope, and values lofty enough to capture the imagination and engage the spirit. Dreams grab us and move us. They are capable of lifting us to new heights and overcoming self-imposed limitations.

Dreams, unlike goals, aren't limited by what you think can or cannot be done or by what your rational mind tells you is or isn't possible. It represents something that you really want, as opposed to something you think you can get.

Dr. Martin Luther King Jr. said, "I have a dream"—he did not say, "I have a strategic plan." The dream of racial equality Dr. King talked about was an elusive, desired state but one that touched people's hearts and evoked a response that altered the history of an entire nation.

To win in our rapid changing, increasingly competitive world it's important to have both dreams and goals, passion and "ration." The starting point of any journey is a dream, a vision of some far-off possibilities. It must be exciting and moving. Once you are enthusiastic about where you are heading, then you set some goals and benchmarks that will help you to get there. When short-term goals become an end in themselves, passion fizzles out.

## ORDINARY PEOPLE, EXTRAORDINARY DREAMS

This country was (and is) built on the dreams of ordinary people who, by following them, accomplished extraordinary things. In the 1930s, for example, A.G. Giannini, although very bright, left school at 14 to take care of his two younger brothers on a small family farm. Later, he got a job working for a bank and had a dream about starting one of his own that would serve "the little guy." He believed that on the strength of many little guys, a national bank could be built. By having the courage to make then unheard of loans for automobiles and appliances, he realized his dream. His "little guys" bank is the Bank of America.

Or consider Peter Seibert's story. A ski instructor and former ski trooper in World War II, Since the age of 12 Seibert had wanted nothing more in his life than to start a ski area. One day, after an exhausting seven-hour climb in deep snow, he reached the summit of a mountain in the Gore Range in Colorado. Staring down at the vast bowls below and at the stunning peaks beyond, Seibert said to himself that it was "as good as any mountain I've seen."

Compared to the hard work that followed, the seven-hour trek was a leisurely stroll. Seibert had to climb mountains of red tape, meet the U.S. Forest Service's stiff requirements, and raise large amounts of capital "from frugal friends and suspicious strangers" to buy land from ranchers and build a village.

"Everybody else thought we were crazy," says Seibert, "but we thought we could do any damn thing we pleased." Seibert's dream is now a reality called Vail.[6]

## TECHIE DREAMS

After being fired from a job he'd held for 14 years, Tom Watson joined a company that manufactured scales, meat slicers, time clocks, and punch cards to sort data. He envisioned that these simple punch cards could start a revolution in information storage. He borrowed enough money to rescue the company when it fell on hard times, and he gave it a new name. "What a big name for a pipsqueak company that makes meat grinders," his son said. It was 1924, and International Business Machines (IBM) was born.

And of course there was the dream of Steve Jobs and Steve Wosniak, 18 year olds working in a garage, of a computer for everyone, out of which Apple was born.

# DREAM MACHINE

A dream can become a magnificent obsession. It can begin in childhood and refuse to go away. We've all had them, but not all of us have had the courage or encouragement to chase our dreams. A fortunate few, captured by their dream early on, have.

Samuel Roger Horchow remembered spending many of his most pleasant days as a child opening mail-order catalogs at random. "Those catalogs were simply dream machines for me. Endlessly capable of taking me far away. That's when I decided that I wanted to be part of the magic world."[7]

That there were hundreds and hundreds of catalogs to complete with never caused a moment's pause to Horchow. He crated his catalog based on his tastes and his vision. Horchow's "dream machine" catalogs are whimsical, farfetched, and passionately personal. You can order a six-foot-long plywood Holstein cow, a Haitian effigy of a clarinet player, or a blown Waterford ship's decanter of full-lead crystal—and with each purchase, the customer gets a small piece of a big dream.

## DREAMS COME IN ALL SIZES AND SHAPES

Your dream doesn't have to revolutionize an industry, win gold at the Olympics, or make a million dollars. It doesn't have to be about work or something that makes a buck. Dreams can be general and abstract, such as wanting to make a difference in people's lives, own your own business, be renowned for your work, or have a loving relationship. Tony Tiano, former president of KQED-TV, the San Francisco public television station, told me his vision is "elusive, like an abstract painting far off in the distance. I can just barely see it. It's something I want. It moves me."[8]

In other instances, your dream can be more specific like John Naber's dream of winning the gold medal, a dream of becoming president of the corporation you work for, or starting your own business. My dream was to write a self-help book, which didn't seem very "realistic" since I got a D in freshman English in college and had never written anything more than a lab report.  And today that almost flunking English student has written 6 books.

Our dreams come in all shapes and sizes. The key is to have something that inspires us to go beyond our limits. Dreams ignite a fire that gives us "genius and magic."

Having a dream, whether it is personal or professional, big or small, realistic or crazy, and *pursuing* it, adds meaning to your life. It gives your everyday activities a larger sense of purpose. And when those you work or live with share your dream, it's doubly exciting.

## PEOPLE'S JOBS ARE TOO SMALL FOR THEIR SPIRIT

If you walk into the headquarters of Patagonia, the outerwear manufacturer located in Ventura, California, you'll see employees in T-shirts and bare feet and walls with surfboards leaning against them. "You'd think this was some kind of laid-back California company," says Yvon Chouinard, the company's founder and head. "But these people are comfortable here. They never want to go home. They work till all hours. They love it here because they know what we are about, that we are dedicated to something more than selling clothes and being financially successful.

"Sure, we make products... but our vision is much larger. The vision at Patagonia is about saving the environment. It's about paying rent on the planet. So, we give a substantial percentage of our profits to environmental organizations. It's a compelling vision for our people, one that grabs them. They feel they're contributing to something more than just the bottom line, and are proud of it."

Today, people's jobs are too small for their spirit. As Chouinard says, "They don't want to work for a company; they want to work for a movement, something that has a larger meaning and gives them a sense of purpose about what they are doing."

A compelling corporate vision that resonates with its employees' dreams and aspirations and touches their hearts as well as their pocketbooks inspires people working for it. That type of company will have little attrition. At Patagonia, "People are lining up to work here."[9]

People want more from life than just to go to work and pick up a paycheck. There's a desire for more meaning and purpose. They want their lives, and consequently their work, to matter, to be a part of a larger vision, and they want to feel they contribute to it. Companies need to create visions that go beyond the notion of being "number one" if they want to attract and retain a spirited work force.

# DON'T BE REALISTIC

In the "real world," dreams are not taken seriously, and often squelched. The President of a large printing company told me of a talk he had with one of their bookkeepers. Though she hadn't finished high school and English was her second language, she was undaunted. Her dream was either to have her own company or become the controller of his company.

Out came the fire hose! The executive, representing "the voice of reality and experience" and ignoring her "passion" cautioned, "You do have good bookkeeping skills but you ought to set your sights on something that's more within your reach, something a little more realistic." Angered by this she quit the company a month later to pursue her dream.

What did she do? She started a bookkeeping service for small companies owned by people speaking English as a second language! Restaurants, laundries, tailors, retail stores, and gas stations were her niche. Today, her business has expanded, and she has five offices in Northern California.

We don't know what is realistic or unrealistic, or what someone is capable of if she is passionate about fulfilling her dreams. Or as this woman told me; "sometimes we're better off if we aren't realistic."

# CREATING LIMITS

I was talking to a group of bankers recently, and afterward, a vice president posed a typical question: "What if I'm a coach of an Olympic hopeful whose dream is to become an Edwin

Moses or a Michael Phelps, but I know that he hasn't got the ability to achieve that dream? Isn't it my job to prevent him from having expectations that are clearly beyond him, of being disappointed? Shouldn't I help him have a clear sense of his own limitations?"

What if you'd said that to a Larry Bird, who couldn't run fast or jump high, or Joe Montana, who couldn't throw as far or as hard as his competition? "You're just thinking with your rational mind," I responded pointedly. "You don't have any idea of what someone else's limitations are!"

We don't have a clue as to what people's limits are. All the tests, stopwatches, and finish lines in the world can't measure human potential. When someone is passionately pursuing his dream, he'll go far beyond what seem to be his limitations. Hall of Fame safety for the San Francisco 49ers Ronnie Lott once said of his teammate Joe Montana, 'You can't measure the size of his heart.' The potential that exists with us is limitless and largely untapped. Bottom line is that *when you think of limits, you create them.*

"One of the most important things in life is the need **not** to accept downside predictions from experts. It's true in interpersonal relationships, just as it is true in business. No one knows enough to make a pronouncement of doom," [10] said Norman Cousins who, at 27, became the editor of the *Saturday Review.*

"The most important thing when you're just starting out is not let the naysayers steal your dreams," says Denver entrepreneur Barbara Grogan. "The world is chock-full of negative people...

They have a thousand reasons why your dreams won't work, and they're ready to share them with you at the drop of a hat. Well, this sounds trite, but you just have to believe in yourself and your ability to make your dreams come true."[11]

## DREAMS ARE THE FIRST CASUALTY

"I'm a big fan of dreams," says acting superstar Kevin Costner. "Unfortunately, dreams are our first casualty in life—people seem to give them up quicker than anything, for a 'reality.'"[12]

In the workplace, personal dreams are disregarded in deference to corporate goals; in our personal lives, dreams fade, as we get older and become more "realistic." We think we know "from experience" what can and can't be done, what we are and aren't capable of, what is possible and what isn't. We then proceed to fire hose our own dreams and those of our kids with what we think is a dose of "reality." Dreams are often the first casualty because we often willingly abandon our own hopes and aspirations in favor of those of the boss.

When I talk to audiences about the importance of having dreams, there is always a sympathetic reaction; it touches something in people. They become quiet. So many of us have lost or given up our dreams, that when I talk about it directly, people have told me it's a reminder of something missing.

## SAVING YOURSELF FROM DISAPPOINTMENT

A typical response when I bring up the subject of dreams; "Dreams? Ha! If I don't make my quota at work, it's going to be a nightmare.!'; 'Dream? I haven't slept in a week, how am I going to dream?; My dream is to make it through the day."

Conventional wisdom has fire hosed many a dream. "Don't get too big for your britches"; "Don't bite off more than you can chew"; and "Get your head out of the clouds" are only a few of the ways dreams are laid to rest.

I was a guest on *Oprah* just after the 1988 Seoul Olympics with five young athletes who had barely missed making the U.S. Olympic team. One woman had been leading in the trials and accidently ran out of her lane, another had lost by one one-hundredth of a second and another by two centimeters. And one had been injured in the Olympic Trials. Although I was on the show as a sports psychologist, I had a similar experience as these athletes, losing by .03 of a second from making it to the Trials.

Talking about the disappointment and frustration of coming so close, Oprah asked, "Now, seriously, might not it have been better to save yourself from the disappointment, to have lowered your sights a little?" It was an interesting question, considering the source—a woman who is one of America's greatest success stories and who, by chasing her dreams, has accomplished incredible things.

"What do you think?" I asked the studio audience. "Would it be better not to chase your dream and avoid disappointment or to have a dream, go for it, and not make it?" To a person, everyone agreed that the far better choice was to have a dream and go after.

Each athlete confirmed this ( and I felt the same way). They talked about how they wouldn't trade the experience of going for their dream for anything. Sure, it had been a major disappointment but chasing their dream had helped them discover something in themselves that, if they hadn't aimed high, they'd never have known existed.

"You must have dreams as well as goals if you are ever going to achieve anything in this world,"[13] said Hall-of-Fame football coach Lou Holtz.

## WHAT IF YOU DON'T HAVE A DREAM?

I am often asked, "What if you don't have a dream?" I answer, "No one is without a dream." We all have hopes, aspirations, visions, and dreams, but we're so busy racing and rushing around that we lose touch with them.

Bank of America's K. Shelly Porges told me she thinks, "The problem is not that people are working so hard because they don't want to look up. They're afraid," she says, "that there is nothing there... no meaning, no purpose, no vision... that they're running on empty."

Remember, when you lose your dream, you lose a little of your potential in the process. As your dream fades, so does your fire. Life gets a little paler. You lose your vigor, confidence, passion, and vitality.

The good news is that even if you have been "running on empty," there are many ways to find your dream, refuel, and begin again.

# STARTING THE JOURNEY

Here are several techniques that can help you to find or recapture your dream and fuel your fire. Deciding to focus on finding your dreams begins a process that can yield amazing results. Take a moment to answer each of the following questions. Let your imagination soar. No holds barred. Don't try to make sense or be realistic. Think about what you really want—something that adds meaning, purpose, and passion to your life. Just thinking about it starts the journey. Write down your responses, and read them back to yourself aloud.

Someday I'd like to_____

_____

I've always wanted to_____

_____

I'd really love to_____

_____

Wouldn't it be great if I could_____

_____

If it were a perfect world, I would_____

_____

If I could do anything I wanted I'd _____

_____

If money weren't a problem I'd _____

_____

Your responses to these questions will prepare the way for you to use many of the following dream-finding exercises.

As you read them, insert yourself into each example, be your own guinea pig, and think as freely as you can... but **beware** of fire hosing yourself!

## THE PERSONAL VIDEOTAPE

Close your eyes, take a few slow, deep breaths, and imagine you're in your home watching a videotape. As the tape begins, see your own name on the screen, and a date five years from now. You have accomplished everything you set out to do, and you are in an ideal situation, living out your dream.

Just watch the tape run. As you view it, don't edit or fire hose anything. Let the tape play itself out unencumbered by your rational mind. Don't analyze it, think about it, or fire hose it. Where are you? What are you doing? How does it feel?

After you have viewed your video, while it is still fresh in your mind, write down a few key words capturing the essence of how you *felt* watching it. Some typical examples are "proud," "independent," "courageous," and "creative." Keep a card on your desk with these "seed" words to trigger your memory of the video and to remind you of your dream.

## REVERSE VISIONING

Imagine you are 85 and looking back over the years. You have lived an active and fulfilling life. You realize that you have gone far beyond what you ever expected you would do or be. As you look back from age 85, ask yourself these questions:

- What did I do with my life?
- What were the significant milestones at age 30, 40 ... 80?
- What qualities did I exhibit?
- How do other people describe my life?
- Do I have any regrets? If so, what are they?
- What would I have done differently?

## HEROES AND HEROINES

Write down the names of your heroes and heroines on a large piece of paper. Don't worry about the strange bedfellows that might turn up. I've seen such a range; you wouldn't believe it — Nelson Mandela, John F. Kennedy, Eleanor Roosevelt, a high school English teacher, Robert Redford, Supreme Court Justice Ruth Bader Ginsburg, Sting, a cousin in the Peace Corps, a parent, Madonna, Michael Jordan, Kobe, and Katherine Hepburn.

K. Shelly Porges tells of a heroine she discovered while attending a tea hosted by the Dean of the Cornell School of Hotel Administration. The teas usually featured successful speakers from the business world, almost all of whom were male. This day, however, the speaker was a woman, the V.P. of sales for a major hotel chain. Porges, a graduate student, was sitting in the audience and saw in the speaker everything she wanted to be—articulate, successful, attractive, and visionary.

While Porges was listening to the speech, she began daydreaming, putting herself in the speaker's place and thinking, "What would I say if I were speaking to this group?"

Years later, Porges was invited to the dean's tea as the honored guest and began saying, "You won't believe this, but I began preparing for this speech seven years ago."

What are the *qualities* that your heroes and heroines embody? What is it about them that attracts you? Which of their qualities have you developed in yourself and which have lain dormant waiting to be awakened?

Visualize yourself having these qualities. How do you look? What are you doing? What would you do differently right now to exhibit and express those qualities?

Remember that you don't have to do what they did to embody their qualities. If your heroes are Mick Jagger or Venus Williams, you don't have to be a rock star or a tennis player. Perhaps Jagger's swagger or Venus's grace under pressure is the trait you admire and would like to emulate.

## THE MAGAZINE COVER

Imagine yourself as *Time* magazine's Man or Woman of the Year five years from now. What did you accomplish that got you on the cover? Write out the quotes of the people describing you on the cover. What are some key adjectives they use? How many of these key qualities have you already developed?

Find three adjectives *Time* used to describe you. Write them down, and then think about what you will have to do to make those terms accurately describe you now.

# REKINDLING YOUR DREAMS

Many of us have faced temporary setbacks or felt discouraged in pursuit of our dreams. Yet, it always amazes me how quickly we can rediscover our dream and get back on track.

"I'm burned out," a building contractor friend told me. "I wanted to move up North and build houses," he continued. "It's growing like crazy, so there's lots of potential. It's a better environment to bring up my kids, a lot less crowded and materialistic. But I lost a bid on a big parcel of land last year, and I got discouraged. That just seemed to take all the steam out of me. I haven't had a lot of energy since. It's getting tougher and tougher to pull myself out of bed in the morning. I don't know why I keep doing this, but I don't know what else to do."

I steered him back onto the subject of building houses "up North" and living a quieter life. I had him visualize how his life would be. It was amazing! Just talking and imaging it renewed his energy. I could feel his excitement build, as he talked not only of the possibilities of working there, but also of the quality of life. "Why don't you make another trip up there to scout out the area again?" I suggested. He smiled and nodded in agreement. A few weeks later, he was at my door. "I'm moving north! I found an even better place of property than I saw last year."

After a setback, old dreams require some attention to begin working their magic back and refueling our passion. Like blowing on an ember, our dreams can flare up and ignite our hearts at any time.

# KEEP YOUR DREAMS ALIVE

Once you have found your dream or rekindled one you thought was gone, the real work is keeping the dream alive. One way to accomplish this is to keep little reminders of it around you. These will rekindle your fire, and rejuvenate your spirit. Remembering your dreams will put your everyday activities into larger perspective.

A regional sales manager for Hewlett-Packard had a dream of having HP dethrone IBM in his area, with him at the helm. The problem was, as he looked out his office window, he faced a large building with three letters on it—I-B-M!

So, to keep reminding himself of his dream, he took a picture of the IBM building, sent it to an art studio, and had the "IBM" airbrushed away and "HP" put in its place. He enlarged the photo to poster size and put it on his wall. On the new "HP building," he outlined the penthouse suite in yellow pen and wrote "my office." Every day, it graphically reminded him of where he wanted to go and what his dream was.

There are small reminders in every occupation:

The salesman who kept a picture of his dream car, an old reconditioned Corvette, at the top of his sample case, so it was the first thing he saw whenever he opened it

The schoolteacher who began collecting maps of bike routes across the country to serve as a daily reminder of her dream of cycling from coast to coast

Arnold Schwarzenegger, seven-time Mr. Universe, who would go into the corner of the gym every hour on the hour to visualize himself winning the Mr. Universe contest again.

Trish McCall who kept a large map of Italy on her wall to keep reminding her of her family's dream to live in Rome for a year.

These reminders help to keep dreams alive. They add a dose of daily kindling to the fire in our hearts. They re-inspire us and keep us moving forward with  more hope, energy and courage. At the 1988 Democratic Convention Jesse Jackson Jr. eloquently said: "The shame in life is not to fail to reach your dream, but to fail to have a dream to reach."

# 23
# BEYOND TIPS AND TECHNIQUES

Each technique discussed in this book is designed to help develop or enhance a specific characteristic that will enable you to perform in the Peak Zone more often. The reality check, for instance, increases your confidence by teaching you how to overcome fear and stress. It helps transform anxiety into action. **Can-dos** and control checks increase your ability to focus, making your actions more effective. Visualization helps to prepare you mentally for a pressure situation and to imprint Peak Zone behavior.

There is no one best technique for everyone and no specific order in which to use these methods. Depending upon your current situation, the performance zone you most often frequent, and which characteristics you need to develop, some of these techniques will be more meaningful and relevant than others. Because situations and environments are constantly changing, and you are continually growing, if you reread this book in six months, other techniques will emerge as valuable to practice.

Though these techniques help overcome the mental obstacles preventing Peak Zone performance, this book is about more than a variety of techniques. A technique isn't magic. It can't create something out of nothing. What it can do is facilitate the emergence of what is already there.

A technique is like a key. It opens a door, allowing you to see what's behind it. The performance zone techniques in this book will help to overcome the fears and doubts that keep your natural abilities locked up. These techniques open the door to your innate potential, which is far greater than you can imagine. They give you a glimpse of what is already inside you and how well you already know how to perform when you have overcome these mental obstacles. That ability is already there. If it weren't, no technique would work. You'd turn the key, and nothing would happen.

Understanding that you already have the innate ability to perform in your Peak Zone is far more important than any technique. This knowledge will teach you to identify with your potential rather than your problems. This shift in your self-concept will change the way you experience and express yourself and how you relate to the world. It will enable you to act from a position of strength rather than weakness; to feel more powerful, confident, and in control of yourself in most any situation; and to continue to grow, change, and transcend previous limits.

Each limit exceeded, each boundary crossed, will verify that most limits are indeed self-imposed, that your innate potential and possibilities are far greater than you ever imagined and that you are capable of far more than you ever thought you were. There are no adequate external measurements for the Peak Zone. There are the internal measurements of joy, vitality, and well-being. There is also the knowledge that throughout your life, you will continue to exceed your own limits and break your own records.

## COURAGE

There is no status quo for the peak performer. In the Peak Zone, you continually learn, grow, and confront new challenges. It is not surprising that the last characteristic of peak performers is courage. It takes courage to change, to confront your fears, to break familiar habits, and to stick with what you believe, though it might not always be easy or comfortable.

It takes courage to commit to your own deepest desires, to play your own game, and to "go for it" in whatever you choose. Ultimately, it takes courage to live life to the fullest of your ability, to be the most you can in whatever you do.

As you close the book, recall a past Peak Zone episode. See it in your mind's eye. Feel it. Experience the power in you. Remind yourself that you already have that ability and that the potential is always there, waiting to be expressed in everything you do, wherever you go.

# ENDNOTES

## CHAPTER 1

1    Robert Kriegel, Ph.D. and Marilyn Harris Kriegel, Ph.D., The C Zone: Peak Performance Under Pressure, (New York: Doubleday, 1984), 1.
2    Ibid., 2.

## CHAPTER 2

1    Gary Mack & David Casstevens, Mind Gym: An Athlete's Guide to Inner Excellence, (New York: Contemporary Books, 2001) 83.
2    Tiger Woods, Golf Digest, November, 2006, 40.

## CHAPTER 4

1    New York Times, Business, May 31, 2009, 2.
2    Dr. K. Pelletier, Holistic Medicine: From Stress to Optimal Health (Doubleday, 1979).
3    Ibid.

## CHAPTER 6

1    San Francisco Chronicle, Jan. 8, 1982.
2    Billie Jean King, Billie Jean, Viking Press, 1982.
3    Sports Illustrated, "An Image in Sharp Focus," May 31, 1982.

## CHAPTER 7

1    Fast Company, March 2005, p. 30.
2    Ms. Magazine, October 1983.
3    Luciano Pavarotti, A Life in Seven Arias, PBS, September 2008.
4    The New Yorker Magazine, August 28, 2006, p. 38.
5    Newsweek, January 31, 2005, p. 51.
6    New York Times, Section 2, October 2, 2007, p. 010.
7    Ibid

8   Sports Illustrated, July12, 1982.
9   New York Times, July 26, 2009, p. 8.
10  Golf Digest, August 2006, p. 100.
11  Personal interview, September 2, 2007.
12  Sandy Linver, Speak and Get Results, New York: Simon & Schuster, 1983.
13  Observations from the the Treadmill ( OFT Union 1976) "An Image in sharper focus" Sports Illustrated, may 31,1982
15  Ibid

# CHAPTER 8

1   T. Peters, R. Waterman, In Search of Excellence, Harper & Row, July 5, 1982.
2   New Yorker Magazine, August 24, 2009, p. 45.
3   The New York Times, July 26, 2009, Sports, p. 1.

# CHAPTER 9

1   Los Angeles Times, August 25, 2006, p. D9
2   San Francisco Chronicle, September 12, 2009, p. B3.

# CHAPTER 10

1   Fast Company, November 1998, p.88.
2   Boardroom Reports, July 1, 1998, p. 13.
3   Buckingham and Coffman, First Break All the Rules (New York: Simon & Schuster, 1999) 137.
4   Fast Company, November 1998, p.88.
5   "The Accidental CEO," Fortune, March 2, 2009, p. 26.

# CHAPTER 11

1   New York Times, July 19, 2009, Sports, p. 9.
2   Los Angeles Times, October 28, 2006, p. D8.
3   New York Times, December 30, 2006, p. Bu11.

# CHAPTER 12

1   Ibid.
2   Ibid.
3   Ibid.
4   Ibid.
5   Ibid.
6   Ibid.

7    Ibid.

8    Golf Digest, August 2006, p. 94.

9    Ibid.

10  Ibid.

11  Ibid.

12  Ibid.

13  San Francisco Chronicle, February 13, 2009, p. D4.

# CHAPTER 13

1    Golf Digest, November 2006, p. 99.

# CHAPTER 14

1    Fast Company Magazine, October 1998, p. 178.

2    Golf Digest, September 2006, p. 44.

3    Golf Digest, August 2006, p. 36.

4    Sports Illustrated, July 12, 1999, p. 98.

5    Ibid.

6    Fast Company, February/March 1999, p. 88.

7    Fast Company, August 1998, p. 80.

8    Fast Company, May 2000, p. 394.

# CHAPTER 15

1    Wriston speech to Washington Business Group on health, Washington D.C., September 18, 1981.

2    Creative Living, 1990, p. 23. P.23

3    Ibid.

4    Boardroom Reports, April 1, 1990, p. 13.

5    Success Magazine, April 1990, p. 47.

# CHAPTER 16

1    YouTube, "Tiger Zone."

2    New York Times, September 24, 2009, Sports, p. 1.

3    Mack & Casstevens, Mind Gym (New York: Contemporary Books, 2002) 136.

4    New York Times, "Lost in the Crowd," December 16, 2008, p. A31.

5    Golf Digest, November 2006, p. 40.

6    Mack & Casstevens, Mind Gym (New York:, Contemporary Books, 2002) 3.

7    Gallwey & Kriegel, Inner Skiing (New York: Random House, 1997) 121.

8    M. Murphy & Rhea White, The Psychic Side of Sports (Big Sur, CA: Esalen Books, 1979).

# CHAPTER 17

1    Sport Magazine, "The Slump: Who Has the Cure?" August 1983.
2    Fortune Magazine, "The Three Minute Manager," March 2, 2009, p. 22.
3    Ostler, "Ochoa Is Leaving the Field Behind," San Francisco Chronicle, October 7, 2007, p. D1.
4    Kriegel & Kriegel, The C Zone (Doubleday, 1984) 85.
5    New York Times, July 12, 2009, p. B14.
6    Kriegel & Kriegel, The C Zone (Doubleday, 1984) 91.
7    Kriegel & Kriegel, The C Zone (Doubleday, 1984) 86.
8    Fortune Magazine, July 6, 2009, p. 48.
9    Kriegel & Kriegel, The C Zone (Doubleday, 1984) 89.

# CHAPTER 18

1    San Francisco Chronicle, September 26, 1982.
2    Kennedy & Jennings, The 15 Minute Heart Cure, (Hoboken, NJ: Wiley & Sons, 2010) 137.
3    Sandy Linver, Speak and Get Results (New York: Simon &Schuster, 1983).
4    Ibid.
5    M. Murphy, The Psychic Side of Sports, (Addison Wesley, 1978).
6    Linver ibid.
7    M Murphy Ibid.
8    Ibid.

# CHAPTER 19

1    Philip Goldberg, Executive Health (McGraw Hill, 1979) 78.
2    Kenneth H. Cooper, Aerobics, (Bantam, 1983).
3    Ibid.
4    Ibid.
5    Fast Company, October 1999, p. 348.
6    Michael Murphy, The Psychic Side of Sports Addison- Wesley 1978
7    Ibid.

# CHAPTER 20

1    Corner Office, New York Times; 7/19/09 P. B2

# CHAPTER 21

1    Joey Reiman, Thinking for a Living (Longstreet, 1998) p. 30.

# CHAPTER 22

1   The San Francisco Examiner, May 27, 1990, p. D3.
2   Personal interview, September 1989.
3   Peter Block, The Empowered Manager (San Francisco, CA: Jossey Bass, 1988) 103.
4   Inc. Magazine, April 1989. p. 42.
5   Fortune Magazine, April 24, 1989.
6   Sports Illustrated, January 30, 1989, p. 76.
7   Spirit Magazine, December 1987, p. 36.
8   Personal interview, December 1990.
9   Yvon Chouinard, Phone interview, March 12, 1990.
10  Success Magazine, December 1988, p. 32.
11  Esquire Magazine, December 1987, p. 102.
12  Vis a Vis, July 1988, p. 58.
13  Mack & Casstevens, Mind Gym (New York: Contemporary Books, 2002) 55.

## DR. BOB KRIEGEL

Ever since Dr. Bob Kriegel co-founded the country's first sports psychology institute in 1972 he's been a trailblazer, developing groundbreaking strategies for keeping ahead of the changes and competition in both the business and sports worlds. The New York Times said his work "spurred a revolution in performance practices." A former all–American swimmer Bob has been a 'mental coach' for many Olympic and professional teams and athletes.

Kriegel, who US News & World Report called one of the countries leading authorities in the field of change and human performance, has been a commentator on NPR's Marketplace program, and did two specials for PBS. He has taught at Stanford's Executive Management Program and co-authored the international best sellers *If it ain't broke... BREAK IT* and *Inner Skiing*, as well as Business Week best seller, *Sacred Cows Make the Best Burgers*.

Breinigsville, PA USA
17 March 2011
257856BV00003B/1/P